12

---

[1] The Indianapolis News – March 28, 1913

The Time of Heroes

The Great Flood of 1913 and the Indianapolis Police Department

By Patrick Pearsey

2018

Forward

The Great Flood of 1913 as it is known, occurred between March 22 and 28th of that year. It affected 13 states and resulted in 650 flood related deaths. Property damage in the amount of $333 million occurred.

The city of Indianapolis had record winds of 66 MPH the evening of Friday, March 21st, which was followed by a violent tornado at Terre Haute, at 9:45 p.m. on the 23rd. It killed 21 and injured 250, the deadliest tornado in state history up to that time. Two consecutive low pressure systems caused heavy rain between March 23rd and 26th.

This event was a major catastrophe for the city of Indianapolis, although as the decades passed, it became remembered by only people affected directly by it.

The focus of this book is the stories of survival in Indianapolis and how the members of the city's police department responded to it. I've created a chronological time line of events from accounts from the Indianapolis Star and News newspapers.

The Great Flood of 1913 is mainly known for the devastation it caused in the section of Indianapolis known as "West Indianapolis", but as will be shown, it affected a vast part of the rest of the city and surburban neighborhoods, primarily the ones below:

- West Indianapolis
- Stringtown, now known as Hawthorne.
- Haughville
- Cerealinetown (where IUPUI is now)
- Mapleton-Fall Creek
- Riverside
- Area bounding Fall Creek from 10th Street to 26th Street
- The village of Broad Ripple, north of the city in 1913 but now a part of Indianapolis.
- Dog Town, on the far south side east of White River, now called Frog Holler.

3   William Ted Riley, 2nd from left, Belt Railroad.

One of the people who lived through this flood was William "Ted" Riley, a conductor on the Belt Railroad. He lived at 1749 West Morris Street. Riley made a practice, as some people did in those days, of keeping a daily journal, recording his observations of the weather and his job on the railroad.

His great-niece Nancy J. Netter has generously submitted his journal during March and April. His record will be included in this history.

---

[3] Nancy J. Netter collection.

[4] Page from journal of William T. Riley, courtesy of Nancy J. Netter.

Friday, March 21, 1913

The city of Indianapolis was swept by a strong storm in the early morning hours of Friday, March 21, 1913. By 6 a.m., winds had gusted to 60 miles per hour, doing a lot of damage in the downtown area.

Six persons, including a police officer, were injured by flying and falling debris. A large electrical sign on the top of the two-story Occidental Building (southeast corner of Washington and Illinois Streets) went over with a crash heard all over town, hanging dangerously over the side of the structure.

At 6 a.m., at central police headquarters at 35 South Alabama Street, Captain George V. Coffin organized a reserve squad made up of night patrolmen and bicycle patrolmen to respond to the high amount of calls for help that were coming in.

He sent men out to guard the downtown stores which had their windows blown out and to warn passerby of downed trolley wires. These were charged with current and would have meant instant death if someone came in contact with them.

It was estimated that it would be several days before all the damage would be repaired. All but a few of Western Union's lines were still working, to the west of town.

George V. Coffin

GEORGE V. COFFIN
Captain of Police [5]

Because he is a principal figure in this major event, the life of George V. Coffin should be examined. He was born May 18, 1875, near Cicero, in Jay County, Indiana to William and Malinda Coffin. At age 11 he was orphaned and was sent to live with his Aunt Rose Carey, on her farm near Carmel,

---

[5] 1913 IPD Yearbook, Lichtenberger History Room.

a small town northeast of Indianapolis at the time.

The Coffin family had for several generations been members of the Society of Friends (Quaker) religion. He enlisted the first week of March, 1899 in Company K of the 14th United States Infantry for service in the Philippines. The regiment was sent to San Francisco. This was during the Spanish-American War. After a stop in Hawaii, George Coffin was in Panay, the Philippine Islands on May 28, 1899.

In 1900, a group known as the Boxers, who were against Christians and foreigners, attempted to take over China. They besieged the capitol of Peking (now known as Beijing). There were hundreds of diplomats from Japan and the western nations in danger here in June.

To meet this threat, two regiments of infantry, the 9th and the 14th, were sent by the United States. The 14th Infantry arrived from Manila on the battleship *Indiana* at Tien Tsin, China, July 27, 1900.

The distance to Peking was 79 miles. Their first major engagement was on August 6th at the Battle of Yangtsun.

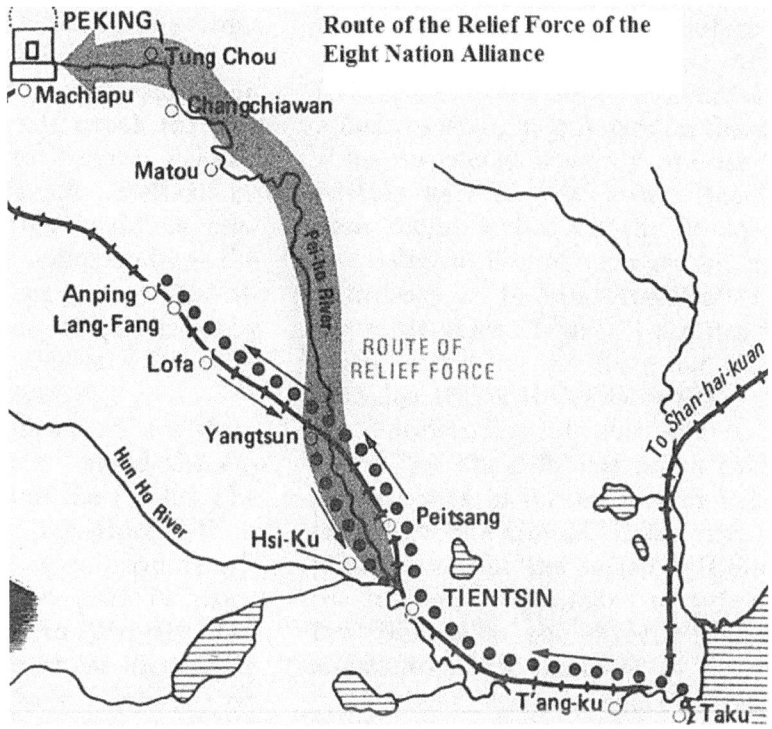

The other nations and the United States, which sent troops to rescue their diplomats were known as the Alliance. Their troops numbered 10,000, the Chinese, 18,000 at Yangtsun. The attack began at 11 a.m. The Americans had used up the water in their canteens and there was none to be had in the intense heat. Dozens of soldiers fell from heat exhaustion and two died of sunstroke.

The Chinese artillery concentrated on the advancing American forces, which had no cover. They also took some friendly fire, which killed 4 and wounded 11. One of the dead, Private Royland Perry, was from Company K. Of the 38 U.S. soldiers wounded in the battle, 7 were from Company K. The action was a victory for the Alliance forces.

The 14th Infantry marched for two weeks in 110 degree temperatures from Tientsin, 80 miles. Early in the morning on August 14, 1900, the 14th left camp five miles from Peking. They marched without opposition until they reached the walls of the city. They then stopped under a pounding of artillery from the ramparts. The original plan was that the American would be assigned a gate but when they arrived there that morning, the Russian forces had already been there and were pinned down by a murderous crossfire.

The 14th U.S. Infantry moved 200 yards south and decided to climb the wall. The walls were about 30 feet tall, 25 feet thick at the base, sloping to 15 feet wide at the top. George Coffin watched as Companies E and H moved forward.

Bugler Calvin P. Titus, 21 from Company E, climbed up the wall, placing his hands and feet into gaps in the bricks. He managed to reach the top and threw a rope down for the rest of the men to use. He later earned the Congressional Medal of Honor.

"I'll Try Sir," a U.S. Army in Action historical painting that depicts American soldiers from the 14th Infantry Regiment scaling the walls of Peking. The Russians were halted by Chinese opposition in the burning gate portrayed on the right of the picture.

Pvt. George V. Coffin led his men up the wall and reached the top. At 11:03 a.m. the American flag was raised on the wall of the Outer City.

They exchanged fire with Chinese troops on the wall, then climbed down the other side and headed toward the Legation Quarter at the base of the wall of the Inner city of Peking. They reached the Legation Quarter about 4:30 p.m., having suffered one man killed and 9 wounded.

George was promoted to the rank of Sergeant for meritorious service after returning to the Philippines from China.

He served there through 1902 during what was known as the Philippine Insurrection. Coffin was an expert with the pistol and rifle. After being discharged from the army, he worked in the lumber camps and grain fields of the west.

Patrolman George V. Coffin

After several years, he returned to Indianapolis, and joined the staff of Central State Hospital for the Insane. He remained on duty during a smallpox epidemic that killed 17 people.

On March 14, 1906, George V. Coffin was appointed as a police officer with the Indianapolis Police Department. He did well, serving as a detective and after several promotions, was one of three men who held the rank of Captain in 1913.

Saturday, March 22, 1913

For Indianapolis, Saturday was a particularly busy 24 hours for its police department. Four men were wounded during that time frame. A shooting occurred in the rear of a barrel house of Max Gordon, 245 West Washington Street Saturday night.

Vance Wilson had sat drinking with a man known only as "Joe" for an hour at the bar, then left out the back door. A minute later a shot was heard and Wilson was shot in the neck. Police found that no one "knew anything" about the crime. Detectives were assigned to the case.

Meanwhile, at the poolroom of James Rains, 550 South Capitol Avenue that night, an argument occurred between William Williams and Robert Thomas. Thomas pulled a weapon and started shooting. Wounded were Indiana Judia, Williams and Samuel Shirley. Williams received four bullet wounds in the head. The suspect fled the scene.

Sunday, March 23, 1913

From William T. Riley's journal: *March 23. Easter Sunday. Rained from 6:30 a.m. until 4 p.m., most all the time extra hard. Quit, then turned warm.*

A murder occurred Sunday afternoon, when Harry Dyson, bartender at the saloon at Senate Avenue and 11th Street, stabbed Elton Pierce, a restaurant owner, to death. They were arguing over a bill at the restaurant. Dyson went to police headquarters and gave himself up to Captain Coffin. Pierce died that night in the hospital.

Benjamin Trimpe and William Kitzmiller

Two IPD bicyclemen, William Kitzmiller and Ben Trimpe, took a call of a fight in the basement of James Hughes' saloon, 2631 West Michigan Street this evening. There, they found no fight but Hughes and 14 men, and some liquor being sold, which was illegal on a Sunday. They had no trouble capturing the men since there was only one door into the basement. The men were charged with operating a "blind tiger".

Meanwhile, back at police headquarters, a call for assistance came in, which was answered by Sergeant Harry Franklin.

"Is this police station?", asked a youngster.

"Yes sir", replied Franklin.

"Well, Alice stole my skates. I want the police to put her in jail." The caller then started crying. Franklin couldn't get anything further out of the crying child.

"And their troubles are just as real and big to them as the other troubles that come over this wire", the police veteran said as he gently hung up the receiver.

Monday, March 24, 1913

From William T. Riley's journal: *March 24. Rained most all day. Warm and night storm at Terre Haute about 15 killed. Omaha, Nebraska (tornado) about 700 killed. All day heavy rain.*

At 3 a.m. on March 24th, the White River had risen to a depth of 16 feet, 11 inches, short of the previous high reached in 1904 of 17 feet, 18 inches.

IPD Motorcyclemen George Stone and Andrew Pressley, both of whom would work in the flood zone.

At police headquarters, located at 35 South Alabama Street, Walter H. Lancaster staggered in at 3 a.m. and asked to speak to someone about a complaint. Lancaster informed Captain Leonard Crane that a police motorcycleman named George Stone was one of three men who assaulted him several weeks earlier at the Brighton Beach roadhouse. This matter was referred to Superintendent Martin Hyland.

C. L. KRUGER
Captain of Police

Captain Christian Kruger, in charge of day shift at police headquarters, instructed his patrolmen to watch the streams in their districts and raise an alarm as soon as they noticed any signs of danger. He also kept

---

[6] 1913 IPD Yearbook, Lichtenberger History Room.

two lifeboats and a squad of men to operate them in readiness.

Just before noon, the situation became worse, as water that was blocked by the Washington Street bridge rose until it cut into the banks on either side of the river, flooding tenements. IPD called out its police reserve with boats.

Monday, March 24, 1913, 12 p.m.

At noon, Captain Coffin led a squad to direct the rescue work going on west of White River around Washington Street. He went west, along the river, assisting here and there.

Mounted Patrolman Hanford Burk

His squad of mounted police and police officers went through the threatened area of "west Indianapolis", on the west side of the White River. They warned residents of the danger and were met with laughs, while others started packing. Other mounted officers who were warning residents here included Charles Metcalfe and Hanford Burk.

Sergeant Charles Metcalfe on "Lew Cooper."

The residents who did evacuate had nowhere to stay. Some did go to the homes of relatives and friends. This was one of the poorest sections of town, mostly common laborers who didn't want to impose on other poor families. They crowded into saloons or stores. The ones who stayed realized they had no place to go in many cases.

Monday, March 24, 1913, 8 p.m.

At 8 p.m., the Weather Bureau issued a report in the evening that there was no

---

[7] 1913 IPD Yearbook, Lichtenberger History Room.

hope that the rains would end. They said that 1.71 inches of rain had fallen in the preceding 24-hours and the rainfall continued. The temperature was expected to fall.

GREENE HAGERMAN,
Sergeant of Police.

8

The Indianapolis Star stated that danger was not imminent. This was based on the

---

[8] 1913 IPD Yearbook, Lichtenberger History Room.

findings of an inspection party sent out from police headquarters consisting of Sergeants Green Hagerman and Harry Franklin.
The men first inspected the levees at Raymond Street, where it had been reported in the evening that water was threatening to burst through. They found no danger.

Hagerman and Franklin moved along White River north, to Michigan Street and saw the high water mark from six to fifteen feet below the levee or bank line. There was one exception – at New York Street, where the water was rising slowly.

The policemen at this time aided the families of Augustus Shenk and Charles Kissel whose homes were in danger of being flooded. They helped them to places of safety. They also warned the people in the neighborhood of the danger, who slept the remainder of the evening on the second floors of their homes.

A rescue 9

Sergeants Hagerman and Franklin then went south, to Morris Street. There they rescued a Mr. Charles Kiler, age 69, who lived in a house boat at Morris Street and White River. With great difficulty they reached the boat and rescued the elderly man and sent him to the hospital.

Sergeant Hagerman reached for a nearby Gamewell patrol box to call into headquarters and was struck by lightning,

---

[9] From "Twelve Views of the Indianapolis Flood of March 1913" published by C.A. Tutewiler, authors possession.

which traveled over the wire and knocked the receiver from his hand. He was not badly injured, although another police officer had been killed in a similar accident in 1911.

LEONARD CRANE
Captain of Police

10

Captain Leonard Crane of IPD, when he arrived for work at night, sent a squad of men to the banks of the White River. The

---

[10] 1913 IPD Yearbook, Lichtenberger History Room.

river was patrolled on both sides from 10th Street to Morris Street.

Patrolmen James Black and Michael P. Flaherty, whose beat included the area south of Military Park (near West Ohio Street and North West Street) began sounding the alarm in the West New York Street lowlands, while water steadily came closer to their homes. This was on the east side of White River.

Tuesday, March 25, 1913

From William T. Riley's journal: *March 25. Warm, rained most all day and night. C.C.C. St. Louis Division washed out at Harding Street and Belt. Still raining at 7 p.m.*

Tuesday, March 25, 1913, 2 a.m.

About 2 a.m., a part of the retaining levee along West New York Street gave out, releasing a torrent of rushing water into the surrounding lowlands. Next, water from the Washington Street area flowed north and met the water from the broken levee, making the flood waters quickly rise.

Patrolmen Black and Flaherty, who had no trouble getting the people close to White River to evacuate, found it was difficult to get people farther from the river to leave their homes for safety. Having weathered many a flood, they refused to leave, despite water near their porches. They refused to believe the White River was an imminent threat.

The first family ordered out by the two patrolmen was that of Clyde Warman, his wife and two children of 225 Beauty Avenue. They called a boat from police headquarters for them. The police department's emergency corps were sending boats to different parts of the city to make similar rescues. Black and Flaherty also carried 80-year old Phillip Reichert, an invalid, from his home at 230 Beauty Avenue.

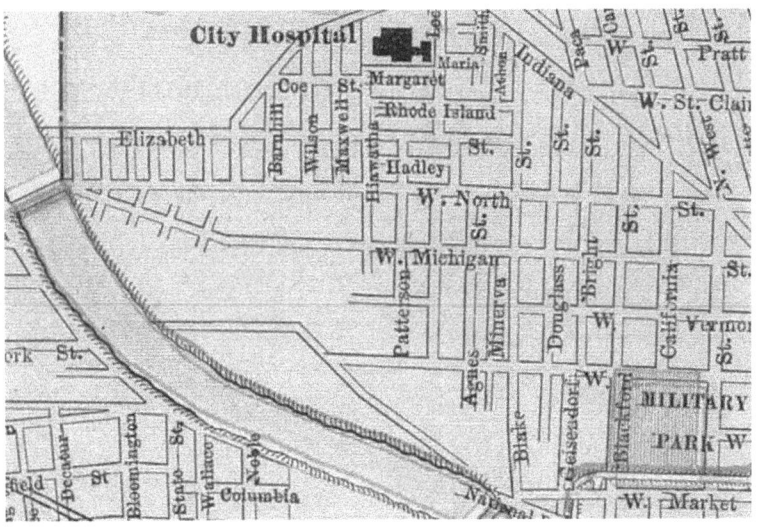

Flood zone was west and north of Military Park to West North Street.

Over 100 families on New York Street, Beauty Avenue and Hansen Avenue were forced out of their homes. The police rescued many of them. Mrs. Fred Shaw, who was bedridden, was taken from her home at 366 Beauty Avenue in a boat by Bicyclemen Andrew Clary and Walter Coleman, to the emergency hospital and then again, later to another location. On the west side of White River, Washington Street was completely flooded.

In the New York Street lowlands, Bicycleman Clary found himself carrying a 200-pound man, wearing a silk hat and fur coat, half a block, knee deep in water, from the police boat. The man refused to have his clothing ruined.

Dogtown Floods

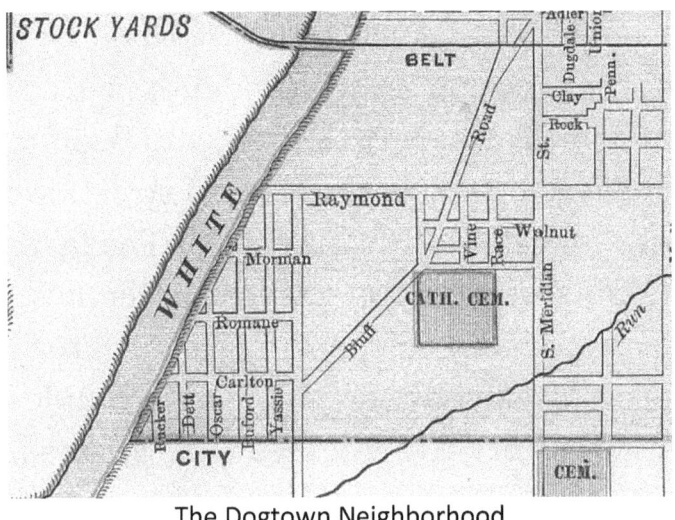

The Dogtown Neighborhood

The neighborhood known as "Dogtown", bounded by South Meridian and Raymond Streets and Bluff Avenue and Pleasant Run creek, had been protected so far from the flood into Tuesday. Located over 4 miles south of downtown Indianapolis, it was guarded by two levees and the Belt Railroad to the north.

The Raymond Street Bridge went down at some point and it was quickly followed by a levee breaking on Pleasant Run. Then a levee broke near Bluff Avenue about 1 p.m. Tuesday, followed by the washout of the

Belt Railroad's elevated track. Many truck farmers were flooded.

Water averaging six feet in depth poured into homes as surprised residents fled for their lives. Among the flooded streets were Daisy Street and Bluff Avenue. The last residents, reluctant to leave their homes, evacuated early this morning. This area was overlooked by the public for a couple of days. Seventy-five families were affected.

Tuesday, March 25, 1913, 5 a.m.

About 5 a.m., water from the White River began flowing into the town of Broad Ripple, what is now a northern neighborhood in Indianapolis.

It took two hours for water to pour over the levee between the Monon Bridge and the canal there, which drove over three people out of their homes. They were forced to take refuge in the Masonic Hall and a schoolhouse. The northern half of town was flooded. The southern half seemed to be in imminent danger as well.

[11] Flood damage at Broad Ripple.

John Rauch, Marion County clerk, who was an officer of the Home Circle Pleasure Club, owned a clubhouse above Broad Ripple. When he heard that the grounds were under water, he became upset and called "Bill", the custodian and ordered him to "stake the building down." By then the water was near the roof and "Bill" didn't obey his instructions.

Miles of low land to the west of Kentucky Avenue, along Eagle Creek, was covered by from three to eight feet of water. There was

---

[11] *The Indianapolis News*, March 27, 1913. Indiana State Library microfilm

nobody left by dawn living here and only the roofs of some homes were above water.

West New York Street, March 25, 1913.

Police made a command decision to make the home of Jesse Collins, 1136 West New York Street, which was a block from the flood at dawn, into a temporary hospital. By 6 a.m. however, water was at the porch steps and some people were being moved farther away from the flood zone. Women

---

[12] West New York Street, Indianapolis, Ind. March 25, 1913 Indiana Historical Society, P0391

and babies were wrapped in blankets and carefully evacuated east.

P0391_BOX15_STREET_SCENES_FLOOD_OF_1913_06
13

Note: This resembles a photograph that appeared in the Indianapolis News on March 26, 1913, which was identified as a water-bound Street car in west Michigan Street, near Hiawatha Street (east of the White River).

Captain Coffin received word from IPD Sergeant William Milam, 57, who lived at 1558 West New York Street, that he needed food and water. Coffin sent a volunteer assistant, William Harryman, in a boat to

---

[13] Car on West Michigan Street, Indianapolis Flood 1913
Indiana Historical Society, P0391

Milam, with an order to report at once to him, to assist in rescue work.

Milam told Harryman he refused to get in a boat, but wanted food and water. Upon hearing this, Coffin sent a second boatman to Milam, with a second order to report for duty, which was also refused. A jug of water was left with Milam. After the flood receded, Milam would face Captain Coffin.

There were three families living in the bottoms area near Indiana Avenue at Fall Creek who were rescued early Tuesday by IPD Patrolmen Claude Powers and Alvin W. Perry. Their houses were completely surrounded by water. They borrowed a horse and carried the women to safety on its back.

After initially being told there were no boats to be found, police department officials located a number and used trucks to haul them from the old Canoe Club, near 30th and Riverside Drive.

Construction of Boats

When the flood was reaching its height Tuesday night into Wednesday morning, calls for help came in constantly, at a rate of 12 an hour.

The City of Indianapolis, principally the police department, needed to acquire a fleet of small boats of any size or type, immediately when this disaster began.

The IPD called out its police reserve with boats. Superintendent of Police Martin Hyland sent trucks to every place that might own a boat and fifty were requisitioned. A call for boats was issued by the early afternoon of the 25th.

One business receiving the call was the G.H. Westing Company, local distributor of Mullins canoes and rowboats. They responded with a new Mullins steel motor boat, rowboats and canoes, a total of 37 boats. Due to logistical problems, Mr. Westing arranged to have the motor boat transported to West Michigan Street for immediate use.

Westing had a number of men in his shop who could run a gasoline motor but none of them had experience handling a boat in choppy waters. Billy Teubner, who was now a representative of the Hendee company, came into Indianapolis to help the G.H. Westing Company at a big auto show at the Coliseum, volunteered. He was a renown racer of Indian motorcycles. He knew how to handle a gasoline engine and a boat. He was wearing a slicker and boots.

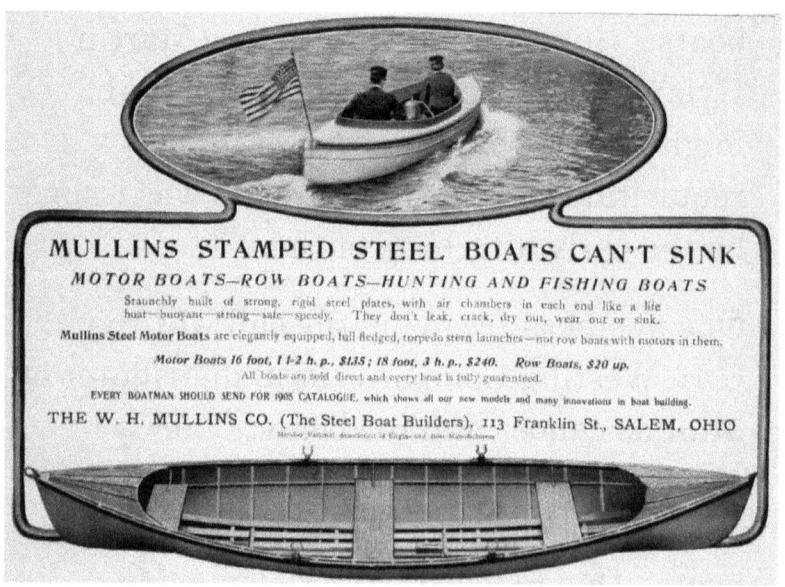

1905 ad for a Mullins Steel Boat.

As Teubner readied his boat for launching, surrounded by a crowd of spectators, a tall man stepped forward. "You'll need someone in there to help you, I'll go."

This was Cass Connaway, Indianapolis attorney. Connaway had experienced boat trips for pleasure at his summer home above Broad Ripple, but this would be different.

The two men battled the waters of the White River all that night until noon the next day. They dodged floating houses, sheds and huge logs while carrying people to safety.

There were experienced boat builders who called at police headquarters, offering their services. They were T.W. Brydon, W.C. Brydon, T.B. Brydon and Joe McKay. Police sent them to the Capitol Lumber Company yard on Massachusetts Avenue. Superintendent Hyland asked several lumber companies to put their men to work building boats.

Tuesday, March 25, 1913, 7 a.m

At 7 a.m., Captain George V. Coffin sent a corps of men with a boat to Brighton Beach roadhouse on West 18th Street, where several families were reportedly in danger due to the White River rising rapidly.

Sergeant Harry Franklin

Sergeant Harry M. Franklin of the Indianapolis Police Department had served

---

14 Lichtenberger History Room.

in 1898, in Company H, of the 158th Indiana Volunteer Infantry, during the Spanish-American War. He was a long time member of the Indiana National Guard when he was appointed to the Indianapolis Police Department. His job there was as drillmaster and he trained the IPD bicyclemen and officers mounted on horses in military order.

Early on Tuesday, March 25th, Sergeant Franklin used his motor boat to remove several hundred people from their homes, although many refused to leave. He worked all day and into the night Tuesday.

The Board of County Commissioners placed all available bridge, carpenter and repair gangs on duty with instructions to protect the county's bridges. Riley Lewis, county carpenter in charge, had the men go from bridge to bridge, pushing away debris piling up against them. The hardest task was clearing it away from the Raymond Street Bridge over White River and the Morris Street Bridge over Eagle Creek.

Mayor Samuel Lewis Shank

The Mayor of Indianapolis, Lew Shank, appealed to Governor Samuel M. Ralston for the State Militia to patrol the city. He ordered detachments from companies A, C and H of the Second Indiana Infantry to patrol in the flood districts of town.

Ralston also directed that the militia quartermaster provide 100 cots to the Volunteers of America, which was aiding flood victims in Indianapolis, as well as blankets and bed sacks to Broad Ripple.

---

[15] 1913 IPD Yearbook, Lichtenberger History Room.

They were to be used for the refugees then staying at the Masonic Hall and the school there.

In downtown Indianapolis, the city was giving refuge at Tomlinson Hall, across the Street from the County Court House to flood victims. An estimated 150 people were given hot coffee, milk and sandwiches and a gasoline stove to dry their clothes with on Tuesday.

Businesses such as the Hazelton Hotel, who said they would house 65 people at no cost, and banker S.E. Kiser, who opened his doors, were but a sample of how the people of Indianapolis showed their generosity.

Pearl Street, March 27, 1913.

A police patrol rescued a woman and child named Kochel, of 929 West Pearl Street (near the east bank of White River) and took them to the hospital.

Police rescued Mrs. Albert Berneke of 206 Bright Street and her children. Her husband was at present jumping into waist deep water to rescue two dozen of his prize chickens and carry them to safety.

---

[16] Pearl Street West Indianapolis, Flood March 27, 1913 Indiana Historical Society, P0391

Tuesday, March 25, 1913, 9 a.m.

The government river gauging station's last measurement in the White River at 9 a.m. was 19.6 feet, topping the record for Indianapolis of 19.5 feet, April 1, 1904. The gauge was then surrounded by water and no further measurements were possible. The Weather Bureau's latest report on March 25th said the past 48-hours of heavy rains would continue for another 24-hours and that flooding was expected.

FLOOD VIEW AT RIVERSIDE

17

Tuesday, March 25, 1913, 10:30 a.m.

A section of the canal levee near the north end of the Riverside bathing beach broke at 10:30 a.m., allowing a torrent of water from the White River to rush through the 100-foot opening. This flooded Riverside Park, at 30th and White River, home of the Riverside Amusement Park.

Within an hour this date, the White River grew to monstrous size, a mile wide. The

---

[17] *The Indianapolis News*, March 26, 1913. Indiana State Library microfilm

oldest residents of north Indianapolis said they had never seen a sight like it.

Flooded roller coaster in Riverside Park.[18]

---

[18] Repository: Library of Congress Prints and Photographs Division Washington, D.C. 20540 USA

Riverside Park above, was near West 30th Street, a popular place for recreation.

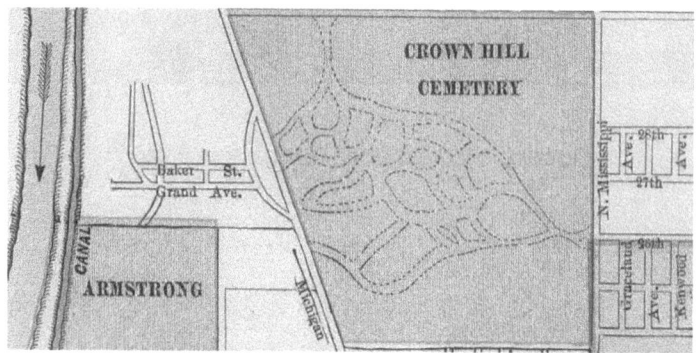

Map of the area of Riverside Park, which was north of Baker Avenue, between the Canal and Michigan Road.

---

[19] Riverside Park, 1913 Flood. Indiana Historical Society, P0326

The levee along the White River south of Washington Street broke in several places this date, along Bluff Avenue and at Raymond Street. The railroad company assigned a large force of its men to repair these breaks and build the levee up with sand.

Another four or five feet was added to its normal height. It was well known that a breech along this section would be catastrophic to "West Indianapolis", to the immediate west.

Indianapolis Water Company's Pumping Station.

Also at 11 a.m. the Fall Creek levee failed, putting the Indianapolis Water Company's pumping station grounds under water. They issued a boil order as a result. For the first time in the history of Indianapolis, the water supply was completely shut off at noon, as the Indianapolis Water Company's Riverside pumping station was flooded and damaged. Water Company workmen had been trying to shore up the levee since the night before, trying to protect the pumping station. When the levee failed, they were marooned. Boats from the police department were sent to 10th and Indiana Avenue under the command of Patrolman Charles O. Johnson, and rescued the men on the levee.

Johnson picked up a dog owned by Al Halfrich, veteran water company employee just before getting into the boat. They were the last to leave. The dog was placed on the bridge with the others.

An estimated 20,000 citizens had gathered throughout the day to watch the flood waters rush underneath the Washington Street Bridge. Just before noon, the water was forced back by the bridge.

It reached a weak point in the bank on the west side of the bridge and broke through. This water rushed down both sides of West Washington Street for two blocks, flooding tenement houses.

Water flowed into the West Washington St. street car power plant, located in this area on the south side of the Street. An extra force of men assigned here bailed with pumps and buckets until 11 a.m. when the fight was given up.

The power plant shut down at noon. Since it was the last of the company's power plants operating, all street cars in Indianapolis stopped running at this point. The Citizens Gas Company plant shut down as well.

Operations in Stringtown

Four blocks of houses submerged in West Washington Street

[20]

"Stringtown" was the name for the neighborhood along the north side of West Washington Street from the river west, to Miley Avenue.

Captain George V. Coffin rowed a police boat to remove a family from a roof top and found other families on other roofs. He kept

---

[20] From "Twelve Views of the Indianapolis Flood of March 1913" published by C.A. Tutewiler, authors possession.

working all day, as the flood waters rose. At some point, he found he was just going to stay on this side of the river. Soon, he would not have a choice.

One officer who had been rescuing people on the east side of the White River on March 25th, crossed over into the west side at some point to assist Captain Coffin. This was Patrolman James Black. He stayed there when the river rose to the point where there was no going back. He was in charge of the refugee center set up at School No. 16.

While there, Patrolman Black spent an entire night guarding a physician who was suicidal. He spent 24-hours guarding this man to prevent him from acting on his temporary insanity.

Patrolman John F. Repp

Patrolman John F. Repp was already on the west side of the river when the flood struck. He was in charge of patrolling the numerous saloons in this area. He passed along Captain Coffin's orders to the saloon owners, which were obeyed.

During Tuesday night, Captain Coffin allowed the saloons to remain open all night because many of the sufferers were in need of stimulants.

The Washington Street Bridge it was still standing, but traffic was suspended except when necessary. Policemen were stationed to guard each end before noon and were forced to fight to keep back the spectators. Throughout the afternoon, West Washington Street, west of the bridge, continued to flood, eventually extending to the 1800 block west.

21   The 1200 hundred block of West Washington Street. Close-up of this photo shows a rescue boat in action.

---

21 The Indiana Album: Barbara Stevens Collection.
22 Ibid

23

West Michigan Street, March 25, 1913.

---

[23] West Michigan Street Flood. Indiana Historical Society, P0326

Fall Creek Spills Over

Patrolman James A. Johnson

During March 25th, another area surrounded by water stretched from Northwestern Avenue (now known as Doctor Martin Luther King Jr. Street), starting two blocks north of the Fall Creek Bridge and running to the area of West 26th Street.

This neighborhood contained about 40 buildings, including grocery and drug

---

[24] Lichtenberger History Room.

stores, saloons and other businesses, as well as residences. Travel by boat was the only option left. Living in two homes at Northwestern Avenue and Myrtis Street were IPD Patrolman James A. Johnson and his father. They were the last residents to move their furniture in moving vans.

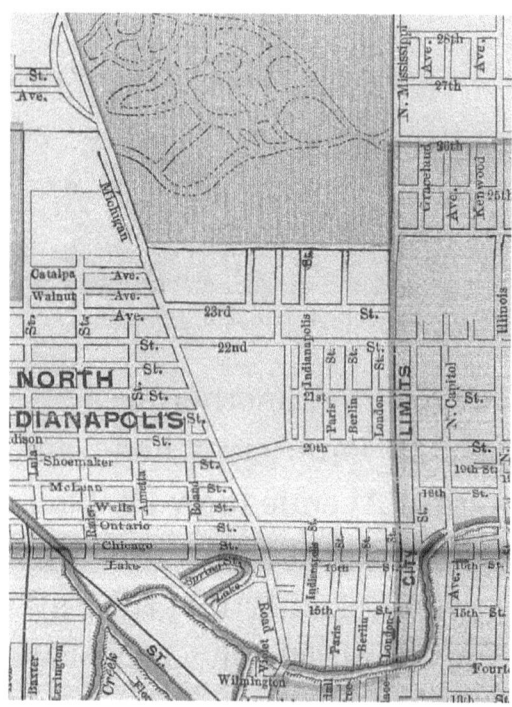

The flood zone extended from the Michigan Road Bridge (now called Doctor Martin Luther King Jr. Street) to West 26th Street, a distance of six blocks. Everything between there was inundated.

ALBERT RAY,
Sergeant of Police.[25]

In the early afternoon, Sergeant Albert Ray of the police department, who was in charge of the area around 30th Street and the Fall Creek, pleaded with residents of this neighborhood to put their possessions in the attics and top floors of their homes and to leave while there was still time. His pleas did not persuade them.

---

[25] 1913 IPD Yearbook, Lichtenberger History Room.

"I cannot see these people risk themselves and their property in this manner", he said. "And they refuse to obey my commands. Commands don't go in a crisis of this kind and I am at my wits' end to make them understand what is to be done. It would be almost impossible to remove them during the hours of the night."

Tuesday, March 25, 1913, 2 p.m.

Flooding at 30th Street and College Avenue.

---

[26] lood in Indianapolis at 30th and College, 1913 Flood Indiana Historical Society, P0326

There was an unexpected break in the levee of Fall Creek, north of 30th Street just after 2 p.m. It flooded the residential neighborhood between Illinois Street on the west, College Avenue on the east and 30th Street on the north. Damage was limited to the north side of Fall Creek. Within 15 minutes, water two feet deep swept through the neighborhood and preventing traffic in and out of the area.

Interurban car tracks washed out on Fall Creek near College Avenue Bridge. [27]

---

[27] Engineering News Record, Vol. 69, p.873, April 24, 1913.

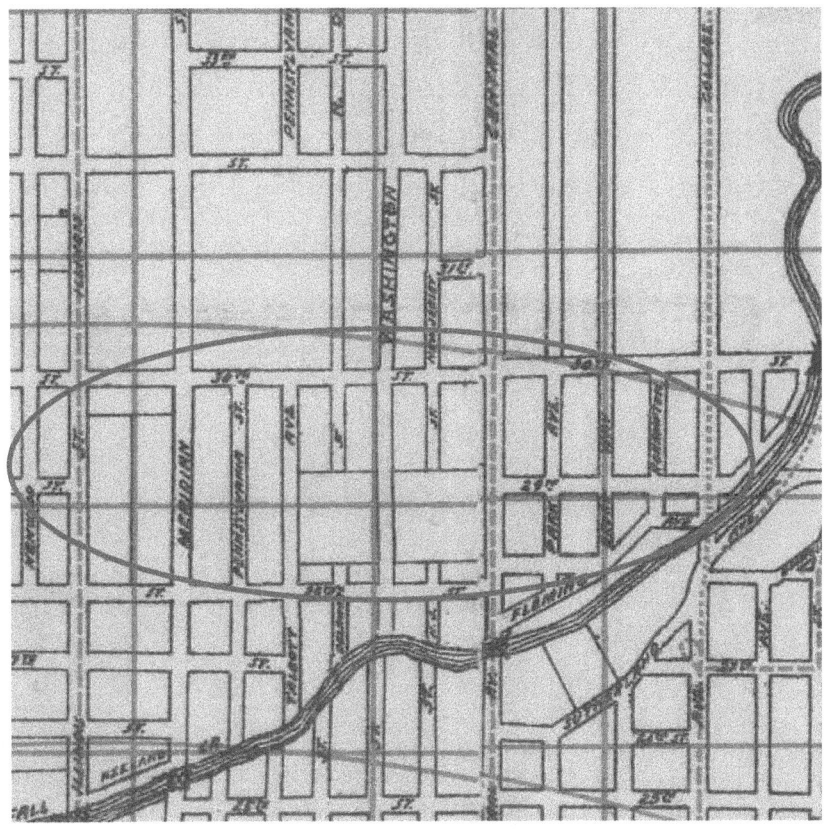

Flood zone within blue oval.

An estimated 5,000 people were made homeless by this flood on the north side of town. This area was a cornfield during the last big flood in 1904. After that, a levee was built – which failed this date. The water swept through the levee breaks across Central Avenue, Alabama and New Jersey Streets, then found its way back into

Fall Creek two yards east of Meridian Street. This current had pounded the north bank of the stream, which led to the failure of the bridge. About sixty people were rescued by police boats.

Police keeping crowds back on the Indiana Avenue Bridge.

The rising level of Fall Creek caused it to flood the area to the west and north of the Indiana Avenue Bridge over it early in the afternoon this day. Every home in the

---

[28] Keeping Back Crowds, Indianapolis, March 1913. Indiana Historical Society, P0326

district was flooded to the east and north of the Indiana Avenue Bridge (above). The residents had little time to flee and many were evacuated by boat.

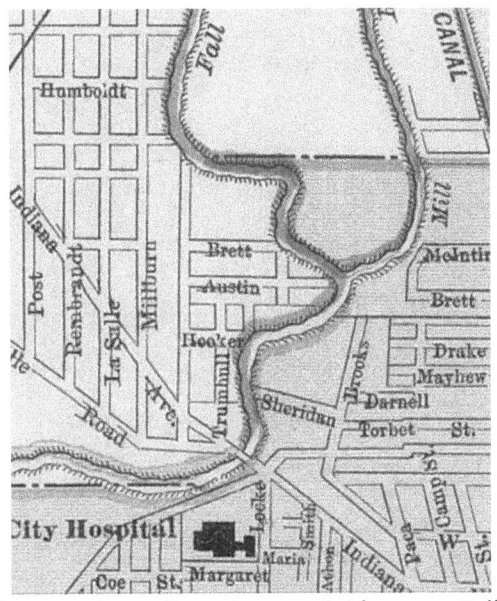
Map showing the Indiana Avenue Bridge over Fall Creek.

16th and Montcalm

Previous page: George Foree (inset) took these photographs during the Flood of 1913 from his home at 1338 Montcalm Street, which is pictured at bottom. They were among his possessions and are generously published for the first time with the permission of his grandsons, John, Jim, and George Peace.

The two men wearing derby hats and overcoats are not as cheerful as they look. They are boating on water which covered their back yard, submerging their automobile and ruining household possessions when the levee broke along Fall Creek during the 1913 flood. Picture lent by Arno G. Siefker, 4024 Moller Road, Indianapolis, who is in the back of the boat. His brother, Fred, is seated in front.

From the *Indianapolis Star* – June 21, 1959

At the time this photograph was taken, Arno Siefker was living at 1412 Montcalm, in the heart of the flooded area near Fall Creek. Photograph was taken by George Foree. This photo was shared by his grandsons, John, Jim, and George Peace.

Two employees of the Indianapolis Traction and Terminal Company proved their dedication on March 25th. Charles Maurey and Earl McClure, linemen for the company, were given instructions to make repairs on some cables that had become entangled near the Emrichsville Bridge over Fall Creek.

Starting out, the men thought they could walk there on Speedway Avenue. They found it was underwater however. Knowing

---

[29] Dayton Daily News Archive. This photograph was taken during the Dayton, Ohio flood of 1913.

that they were told to make the repairs as soon as possible, Maurey and McClure decided to walk their using the cables. They held onto the upper cables while walking on the lower ones.

Indiana Avenue Bridge.

Starting out near City Hospital, they walked ¾ of a mile toward the bridge over Fall Creek at Indiana Avenue. As they crossed twenty feet above the water over the bridge, the poles in that section gave way and fell into the water. The men were

---

[30] Indiana Avenue Bridge, Indianapolis, March 1913. Indiana Historical Society, P0326

thrown over with the poles. They managed to hold onto the cables and made their way to the river. Shaken, they said they'd be back at work Wednesday.

Water over the Bridge

The Indiana Album: Barbara Stevens Collection

[31] Spectators on the Michigan Street Bridge during the flood. The water topped the bridge at some point March 25th.

Some of the Indianapolis public schools were closed during the day Tuesday. One of these students was Naomi Pearsey, age 8, great-aunt of the author. Naomi said that during the Flood of 1913, she was let out

---

[31] The Indiana Album: Barbara Stevens Collection.

early from school. She lived in Haughville, on the west side of the White River.

When she and her classmates got on the Michigan Street Bridge to cross to the west, water started coming over the top. They took off running to get across.

Mary (Conway) Pearsey

Also crossing the Michigan Street Bridge from the east around this same time was the author's grandmother, Mary (Conway) Pearsey, age 23. She told her family that when she crossed, she saw rats swimming over the bridge deck as she fled for her life.

Later observation from a distance showed only one railing of this bridge above water. Michigan Street seemed to be the northernmost boundary of the flood west of the White River, homes north of there not experiencing too much damage.

Rumors, Rumors

Wild rumors were sweeping the city by now. Calls were coming into the local newspaper offices, as well as the police and fire departments. One report said that 50 men were killed in the Kingan packing plant which was located on the bank of the White River near Washington Street, when a building wall by the water collapsed. Another false report said that 1,000 people died in the West Indianapolis district.

A number of reports of rescuers dying in drowning accidents were coming in.

Crisis at the Morris Street Levee

Tuesday, March 25, 1913, 3 p.m.

At the 25-foot high White River levee at Morris Street, a tiny stream of water began to seep through it. Workers plugged the leak with bags of and straw bales, placing telephone poles on top of them. A group of 100 men reinforced the levee.

Morris Street Bridge – 1907 Postcard.

There was a lot riding on keeping this levee intact. On the west side of it was the low lands of "West Indianapolis" where thousands of people lived and worked. This levee had to hold.

Tuesday, March 25, 1913, 4 p.m.

At 4 p.m., while work was being done on the leak on the levee north of the Morris Street Bridge, water suddenly burst through the barricades at the west end of the bridge itself, at the corner of Drover and Morris Streets. This was not expected. When this happened, hundreds of residents of the West Indianapolis lowlands to the west of the breech were busy packing their household items and carrying them upstairs to supposed safety.

Thousands of gallons of water poured through the break, sending residents into a panicked evacuation in wagons, carts, buggies and cars. Up to this time, no official evacuation order had been issued by the city or any other official agency.

Tuesday, March 25, 1913, 5 p.m.

For the next hour after the 4 p.m. break, cars loaded with fleeing residents, drove east across the Morris Street Bridge. Families fought their way through the water by vehicle and on foot, loaded down with whatever they could carry. Like Moses leading the Israelites across the Red Sea in *"The Ten Commandments"* they carried pens of chickens along with furniture, stoves and other household fixtures.

Although it was thought this breech on the south side of the bridge would take the strain off the levee above the bridge, at 5 p.m. the levee was showing signs of failing. All attempts to repair the levee had been abandoned by now.

It was about this time that Mayor Shank notified Fire Company 19 at Morris and Harding Streets the Morris Street levee was breaking. The men went into action, not knowing how long they had to evacuate.

From William T. Riley's journal: *Water up to ties at Abattoir switch at 5:20 p.m.*

Tuesday, March 25, 1913, 6 p.m.

The water level was even with the top of the Morris Street levee at 6 o'clock that evening. Observers waited to see the water go over the top. According to the Indianapolis Star, at 6:10 p.m., the unexpected happened.

Suddenly the water burst through the bottom of the levee, 400 feet north of the bridge. Tons of rock caved in and a 25-foot tall wall of water a half mile wide rushed through the opening. This ripped out the west approach to the Morris Street Bridge.

The crowd of 2,000 onlookers was transfixed by the awesome display of nature. The water shot into Drover Street, toward the doomed houses there.

HIGH WATER IN RIVER AVENUE NEAR KENTUCKY AVENUE

32

Mrs. Ella Fanning, who lived at 909 River Avenue, begged her neighbor, Mrs. Mary E. Smith, 76, of 907 River Avenue to leave and flee the oncoming flood waters. "Oh, I can't," Mrs. Smith said. "My things! They are all that I have in the world! If I leave them they are lost and without them, I, too, may as well be lost!"

As she said this, other neighbors were rushing to escape, taking a few seconds to plead with Mrs. Smith to leave. "I can't! I

---

[32] *The Indianapolis News*, March 27, 1913. Indiana State Library microfilm

can't!" she said in response. She climbed on her bed and waited.

Two blocks away, at 1106 River Avenue, lived Mrs. Mary Pryor, 38. She had been reluctant to leave in the face of the danger to the levee. Mary, who suffered from tuberculosis, had two boys with her. The rest of the family fled.

When the Morris Street levee broke, the waters rushed toward her home and caught them before they could leave. The three of them spent the night in the second floor of their home.

Part of the White River flowed into a neighborhood at Kentucky Avenue and Morris Street, destroying homes in its path. Three thousand families were made homeless due to this break in the levee.

Damage estimates were over $1,000,000. This included a dozen grocery stores, an equal number of saloons and some drug stores that were now under water.

33

---

[33] *The Indianapolis News*, March 26, 1913. Indiana State Library microfilm.

34 The Morris Street levee which caused catastrophic flooding.

There were large factories, including the Puritan Bed Spring Company and the Western Oil Refining Company, were submerged. Twenty-five men, women and children took refuge in the Puritan Bed Springs Company's factory, planning on spending the night. A Lieutenant Ball, who was in charge of a squad of militiamen,

---

[34] From "Twelve Views of the Indianapolis Flood of March 1913" published by C.A. Tutewiler, authors possession.

ordered them to leave, fearing it would be swept away by the flood.

IFD Station House No. 19, 1445 West Morris Street, March 26, 1913 – Photograph from Jim Barrett.

Within minutes after getting Mayor Shank's warning call, the men of Fire Station No. 19 saw water began to flow into the building. By the time the firemen hitched horses to their wagons, the water had reached their waists. Flood waters quickly filled it with over nine feet of water.

35 House in center of River Avenue.

Thirty fleeing residents stayed on the second floor of the home of Morton S. Matthews, at 1133 River Avenue.

Miss Ethel Krouse, of 968 West Pearl Street, was busy preparing for her marriage, scheduled for Monday, March 31st. When she and her mother saw water begin to seep into their home, they started leaving. When the family had gone several

---

[35] From "Twelve Views of the Indianapolis Flood of March 1913" published by C.A. Tutewiler, authors possession.

blocks, Ethel realized she had left her Hope Box containing her white wedding gown behind.

Despite the protests of her mother and sister, she raced back home, wading through the rising water. It was too high and police officers pulled her back. When Ethel returned to the edge of the flood zone, she found her mother and sister gone. Ethel was taken to the Salvation Army in a wet calico dress, all that she had taken with her.

One man who didn't immediately flee was James W. Cline, who owned a saloon at 1102 West Morris Street, corner of Kentucky Avenue. He was busy underneath his automobile making repairs on it when the levee broke.

Several men who were running from the water yelled at Cline but he refused to leave. They last saw him working on the machine as water began creeping up on him. John Brennan saw Mrs. Cline making her way to the railroad tracks, while calling her husband several times. Mr. Cline's fate was unknown the next day.

At 918 Arbor Avenue lived Mrs. Anna Moore and her daughter Miss Nina Moore. Boarding with them was Mr. Harry S. Garrison. The women left the home before the flood waters reached them.

Garrison and some men stayed behind and saved part of the furniture, but were finally forced to wade out of the area, riding on horses the rest of the way. Garrison and Miss Moore would be long parted however.

Johnny Johnson, a machinist at the Vandalia shops, left work at 6:15 p.m., just as water was rushing his way from the White River. He left the Harding Street business on his way home to 338 North Miley Avenue. He started to wade in the deepening water toward the Belt Railroad.

Men who had come from that direction told him that water was coming over the railroad tracks and he wouldn't be able to get home that way. "I've got to get home to my wife—she'll worry" and headed west.

He was last seen on his hands and knees in a half a foot of water, feeling his way along the top of the railroad tracks. He No one saw him again during the flood.

Tuesday, March 25, 1913, 6:30 p.m.

The first part of West Indianapolis to be flooded when the levee broke, was Morris Street, west of the Morris Street Bridge. This picture gives a glimpse of the district under several feet of water.

---

[36] *The Indianapolis News,* March 27, 1913. Indiana State Library microfilm.

A Four Foot Wall of Water

As chaos reigned along Morris Street, 100 men were still trying to shore up the levee ½ mile north of here where Oliver Avenue crossed the White River. They heard a commotion behind them and saw a wall of water four feet tall rushing toward them from the west, on Oliver Avenue. This flash flood didn't come from Morris Street but farther north, when a breech in the levee at West New York Street occurred.

The water first ran down Koehne Street to Washington Street, then turned right and through the Harding Street overpass. Going down Harding Street, it passed over and through two sets of elevated railroad tracks. It then was forced by the Hill on the south side of Rhodius Park to turn east, toward the "valley", the residential district in West Indianapolis.

To get there it had to get past the elevated tracks of the Belt Railroad, which ran in a north-south direction along Harding Street. It was at least 8 feet high according to one account. The tracks acted as a levee, but not for long when the force of the water cut through it.

While the water was charging toward West Indianapolis, two men were trying to warn residents to evacuate this area. One was Edward C. Brennan.

He recalled in a 1957 interview, the city engineer coming to his automobile garage on Tuesday, March 25th. "The White River is 19 feet higher at Noblesville than here", recommending evacuation. A south-sider himself, Brennan went to West Indianapolis with four of his employees to give the warning. Many of the residents laughed in response.

Attorney William P. Reagan was driving back and forth trying to give the warning, but no one was listening. Then he was seen driving fast down Oliver Avenue, toward the bridge, yelling "Here comes the flood!" Behind him was the crest of a two-foot wave from the west.

Edward C. Brennan, who lived at 124 West Raymond Street, drove a motorcycle through Kentucky Avenue, Morris Street, Division Street and other adjoining Streets, warning people to go to higher ground.

He was busy on Oliver Avenue at 6:30 p.m. giving the warning when he looked up to see water coming his direction from both Marion and Oliver Avenues. Brennan said, "I could see it rushing toward us. A crowd of people there rushed through the shallow water already there and got into some buildings."

As described by the Indianapolis News on March 26th –

"FLEE FROM FOUR FOOT TIDE"

"A wall of water about four feet high swept down Oliver Avenue last evening about 6:30 P.M."

The workers at the levee ran for their lives across the Oliver Avenue Bridge to the east side. Residents who lived here did the same. The wall of water began to pile up behind the levee and headed south to meet the flood at Morris Street.

Mr. Brennan spent two sleepless days working from the east end of the Morris Street Bridge, organizing rescue parties. He remembered watching as more than 20 boats capsized and were lost in the 15 MPH current through the streets.

37 The view the levee workers had of Oliver Avenue from the bridge looking west before the wall of water hit.

---

[37] Oliver Avenue, looking west, 1913 (Bass #33058) Cropped.

"The water was backed up behind rows of houses three feet higher than in front, because it couldn't get between them fast enough. A boat would swoop down the incline of water between houses and it was like shooting the rapids on a river", Brennan said.

The rescuers ran ropes from the Morris Street Bridge to surrounding homes because the boats couldn't handle the current any other way.

"We saw a man's arm sticking from a hole in the roof of a house, waving weakly. Inside, after we chopped the roof open, we found two couples. Later that evening, Brennan's boat slammed into the roof of an abandoned street car at McCarty and Division Streets.

Bass Photo Co Collection, Indiana Historical Society

Direction the water came from

---

[38] The Indiana Album: Joan Hostetler Collection.

Oliver Avenue.

[39] Oliver Street, West Indianapolis, March 1913
Indiana Historical Society, P0326

[40] Police boat in Oliver Avenue.

One family trapped in their home at 642 Division Street was that of Thomas B. Wright, purchasing agent for the house of representatives. He took his wife and three children to the attic of their home at midnight. "I have never expected to see such pitiful sights", he said later. They were caught by the 6:10 p.m. flood.

---

[40] From "Twelve Views of the Indianapolis Flood of March 1913" published by C.A. Tutewiler, authors possession.

"Later the big break came at Morris Street and then it mounted to the ceiling of our first floor. Meanwhile I had gone to the barn and brought back a hatchet, saw and hammer. I cut a hole in the roof and we climbed up there. I fully believe that all in the district between the two bridges, who did not escape early in the day, and who lived in one-story houses, was drowned", Wright said.

Shooting the Rapids on the White River

HARLEY REED,
Sergeant of Police.

Walter H.. Cox

Patrolman Walter H. Cox and Sergeant Harley Reed of the police department were said to be the first police officers to reach the West Indianapolis neighborhood. Cox and Reed reached the flooded district as the result of an accident.

---

[41] 1913 IPD Yearbook, Lichtenberger History Room.

They were crossing the White River in a boat Tuesday, March 25th when their craft toppled over. They were carried downstream by the current, but caught hold of an outbuilding that was floating down the water.

They were carried to a point near the Morris Street Bridge and afterward got possession of another boat that was floating down the river, and in that way made their way to the stricken portion of the city. After reaching there they rescued nearly 200 persons.

After dark on the 25th, Sgt. Harley Reed and others went to a lumber yard, where they built five boats.

The Indianapolis Abattoir Company, which was located on high ground, was surrounded by water after the levee broke. Five employees of the company began working from that evening through Thursday, day and night.

Harvey Reed, Elton Hart, Henry Watson, Ralph McIntyre and William Wyman rescued people. They took Mr. & Mrs. John Mack and the Elmer Dauefel family, all living in the 1400 block of Nordyke Avenue, from their homes, in two row boats, Wednesday night. They took provisions to those who refused to leave their homes.

Police Rescuing the Police

Detective K.A. DeRossette   Detective William W. Larsh

William W. Larsh, a city detective who lived just south of Oliver Avenue, at 826 Warren Avenue, found water rushing through the first floor of his home. Larsh managed to telephone police headquarters and said he

---

[42] Lichtenberger History Room.

would be drowned if they didn't come and get him.

He and his family were rescued by IPD Detective K.A. DeRossette who rowed up to his partner's home. "The only reason my family and I escaped was because the boat took the wrong street and came down by our house.

While taking the Larsh family to dry land, they passed the home of Thomas B. Wright, whose wife and three children were taking refuge in the attic to escape the flood waters.

According to Wright, "He yelled at me and I said, 'Sure I want to get out of here.' He took the children first and then came back and got my wife and me. They landed us at the River Avenue (Oliver Avenue) Bridge and we walked across. We went to Tomlinson Hall and there the nurses took care of us. We were soaking wet. They deserve much credit for the work they did for the sufferers. I saved only the clothes on my back."

Aborted Bread Delivery

A pair of men, William Wolf and Dan Smith, headed south of Washington Street Tuesday night with a wagon loaded with 300 loaves of bread sent by the Century Baking Company for flood victims. They got about five blocks south of the Oliver Avenue Bridge when the water got too deep for them.

They unhitched their team and each mounted one of the horses. Smith was thrown twice into a swift current and wasn't seen again by Wolf. Smith managed to find refuge in a home, where he stayed until being rescued Wednesday morning.

"I Want to Forget It"

Coffin moved the refugees he had rescued to School No. 16, located at 1402 W. Market Street. He was assisted in these efforts by Lester Jones, connected to the City Dog Pound and IPD Bicyclemen Charles Gollnisch and Thomas O'Brien. Patrolman James M. Black was in charge of the refugees when Captain Coffin was absent.

During one of his boat trips, Captain Coffin rescued two men. Based on putting various accounts together of what happened, it is believed one was named William Baxter. He had a companion with him.

The companion rowed on the trip to School No. 16. Baxter became violently insane and Coffin had to fight him all the way to the school house. In the boat with them was a mentally disabled youth and a blind girl.

While the fight was going on, the boat capsized. The companion fell overboard and apparently drowned. Later, William

Baxter, a railroad employee, was found marooned in a box car, where he had swum after the canoe capsized. When the rescuers found Baxter, he became violent and had to be restrained. He was taken to the train and after arriving at the Capitol Avenue station, some friends took him in charge.

When asked about this incident, Coffin refused to talk about it, saying "I want to forget it."

After this horrible experience, Coffin rowed to School No. 16 where he found 473 people huddled on the second floor. The school was now surrounded by eight feet of water.

The Saga of Teubner & Connaway

The motorboat of Billy Teubner and Cass Connaway made the first trips west of the street car barns on west Washington Street since earlier in the day, after dark. For the next two hours they piloted this boat and took about 100 children, removed from second-story windows and roofs, to School No. 16.

Repeatedly, loaded with between six and eight children, they would fight the currents, which threatened to capsize their craft. "The cries of the persons caged in those small homes on West Washington Street was pitiful," said Mr. Connaway.

Mr. and Mrs. Charles Goss were rescued from the second story of their home at 536 Arbor Avenue (north of Washington Street) by Teubner and Connaway. They had a pair of canaries.

The husband suggested hanging their cage from the ceiling. Mrs. Goss refused, saying she wasn't going unless the birds went. She waded through the cold water on the second floor and found a sheet to wrap the cage in for warmth. After being taken to the Y.W.C.A., the birds began singing for the enjoyment of the children.

Connaway said during the rescues the people they took on board insisted on bringing with them poodles but drew the line when a man wanted to bring along a big bulldog. They left him and another party rescued both of them.

Teubner said later that on one occasion they found three men floating on a small shed and were numb from the cold. They carried them to Washington Park, the city's baseball stadium and landed them on the grand stand, so they could get back to rescuing the women and children they heard crying for help above the sound of their boat motor.

One woman stuck in Teubner's mind. She was calling out desperately from her second story window for help. They tried everything possible to get to her but several fences separated them. In the end they had to leave, while water continued to rise. Teubner felt she probably drowned.

Tuesday, March 25, 1913, 7 p.m.

By 7 p.m., Connaway and Teubner were soaked to the skin and chilled. They made their way to shore, desiring to go to Connaway's home for a change of clothing.

They were taken by automobile to his home, 311 ½ East Walnut Street on the other side of town. Connaway could not find any dry clothes. All he could find was a tuxedo and a stiff bosomed shirt. They went back to work.

As they got back into the boat, a laborer pushed forward and said, "Here, take this, it'll keep you warm," as he took off his coat and handed it to Connaway. Later, the attorney said, "I would like to meet that man. He had a big heart and he knew when to let it expand. I hope he finds out who I am so I can thank him."

Late Tuesday, Sergeant Harry Franklin was instructed by IPD headquarters to take sandwiches and coffee to all the men, women and children huddling in School No. 16, and to relieve Coffin and his men. Teubner and Connaway offered him their motor boat. They and William Neuker made up Sergeant Franklin's crew for this voyage.

They returned to their rescue mission, this time with Sergeant Franklin directing them. The little motor churned the water furiously, but it was an unequal task. Franklin said that their boat was caught in a current running 40 or 50 MPH and it was all they could do to keep it from capsizing.

The men shot the rapids under the elevated tracks on Washington Street (near Harding Street) at high speed, doing a couple of 360 degree turns, before landing on the shore to check on the engine.

Stories of Survival in West Indianapolis

Lieutenant Charles Barmfuhrer was appointed district patrolman December 15, 1897, February 21, 1906 was made sergeant, and December 27, 1911 was made lieutenant.

43

Among the first responders into the area of West Indianapolis were IPD Lieutenant

---

43 1913 IPD Yearbook, Lichtenberger History Room.

Charles Barmfuhrer and a squad of rescuers. During this evening into Wednesday, they brought hundreds of survivors from their flooded homes. Barmfuhrer was highly regarded within the department.

44 Carrying refugees down Oliver Avenue to landing place.

One dramatic story of rescue was told by Mrs. Alia Streeter, of 1110 Oliver Avenue and Mrs. Ella McKinley. "It was awful", Mrs. Streeter said. "The terror of it! Just to

---

44 *The Indianapolis Star,* March 27, 1913. Indiana State Library microfilm

think that he would not heed the warning given us. And then to see that awful yellow water curling about the house, rising to the first floor and finally reaching the ceiling of our home. We were forced onto the roof. I carried a lamp, which sputtered and then went out. I could not light it. Then the roof of the house started to shake. We knew the foundations were being undermined. Presently we heard shouts from the darkness, and then a light came into sight. I screamed with all my might. Our feelings soared when the light turned toward us."

"One by one my family and that of Mrs. Williams were taken from the roof and put into the boat. As we came to the bridge I could hear shouts and screams all about us, and I am sure there are others back in that old hole. No one knows how thankful I am that we were able to get out safely. I know others were not so fortunate."

When the flooding began in West Indianapolis, Philander R. Gray, 44, 1079 River Avenue got his family ready to evacuate. Mr. John Repass, a grandson, recorded a vivid family account of the events of that night. Philander carried one of his eight children on his shoulders as they walked out of the house. The water was already over the top of the porch steps.

The Gray family waded toward Morris Street, a block away. As they reached it, the current began flowing toward Harding Street in the east. They followed it and walked another block to the Belt Railroad tracks on Morris Street. This was near Fire Station No. 19 which was partly submerged.

The family stepped from the water and were given shelter at the church on the corner of Blaine Avenue and Morris Street. With his family safe, Philander and his son William, headed back to their home to move the furniture upstairs to safety. It was now about 8 p.m.[45]

---

[45] http://www.westindianapolis.org/wp-content/uploads/2010/12/History-Vol-4.pdf

Coffey Street, March 26, 1913.

---

[46] Coffee Street, Indianapolis, After the Flood, 1913
Indiana Historical Society, P0408

Albert Gibney

Albert Gibney, a former member of the Indianapolis Police Department, attempted to rescue his mother from the upstairs of her home at 648 Coffey Street (a block south of Oliver Avenue).

He wasn't able to reach the house and had to abandon the attempt. He did make several rescues along the way. At Ohio and Division Streets he found and elderly man and his wife standing in waist deep water. Gibney got them in the boat and took them to the K. of P. Hall in West Indianapolis, where they received aid.

Betty Blythe, Reporter

The amount of rain measured during the 24-hour period ending at 7 p.m. this evening was 2.58 inches. A total of 5.54 inches had fallen since it began, Sunday morning, March 23rd. It was impossible to measure the White River's height by now but it was estimated at 22 feet.

Betty Blythe, reporter for *The Indianapolis Star*, was on the east side of the White River this day, observing the activity at the Washington Street Bridge with disbelief. She watched a police squad working hard all day, as they had the night before, removing citizens from flooded houses.

A man staggered to get out of one of the boats as it reached the east side of the river. Rescuers reached out for him. "That is Joseph Rodgers, pastor of the Home Mission Church of America," whispered Sergeant Harry Franklin. "He has rescued more people than anybody out here. He has been out in the boat steadily since 4 o'clock this morning."

Samuel Rariden[47]

Rodgers, exhausted from his labors, said "I'll have to quit. I cannot work anymore", being led away with assistance. When the refugees were landed on the bank of the White River, ambulances and any vehicle that was pressed into service by the city, including many that were loaned by private citizens, took these suffering people to nearby hospitals. Sergeant Samuel Rairden of IPD, was one such ambulance driver.

Likewise, the police officers were also worn down by their constant efforts. Some had been on duty all day and night since yesterday. Reporter Blythe was transported

---

[47] Lichtenberger History Room.

in a National motor car, which driver Arthur Beckner managed to ford flooded streets with. He only hesitated when crossing the Washington Street Bridge. "The other side is the place for us", he yelled. "I don't like the noise this bridge makes when one of those overturned houses strike against the piers."

Patrolman William "Bill" Wilson

"Ah, stick with the gang", replied IPD Officer "Bill" Wilson, who had been working 24-hours straight.

Another boat which Ms. Blythe saw arrive, carried an elderly woman. A police officer wearing rubber boots waded out and picked her up. The man rowing the boat yelled, "Hurry, oh, damn it, hurry", to the officer. "Come on with me. There's an old man back there we have to get!"

This was just one rescue sortie among hundreds made by dozens of small boats, maneuvering between all sorts of debris, including houses, crashing into the Washington Street Bridge. Meanwhile, thousands of residents watched the spectacle, being held back by police. Most of these were volunteers.

One policeman at the Morris Street Bridge asked another, "How long are you going to stay here?"

"I haven't any orders."

"Well, just stay all night."

This officer said he hadn't eaten since 6 a.m. that day.

Reporter Betty Blythe closed her story with "The last thing we saw as Driver Beckner turned his car's nose eastward from the West Washington Street Bridge were the tired police officers – with "Bill" Wilson still on the job – sending out the little boats and carrying the women to dry land."

When *The Indianapolis News* was issued that evening, their lead article said that Indianapolis was *"without street car service, water supply, almost entirely deprived of railroad and interurban service, and without a supply of gas in a large part of the city this afternoon."*

All of the streams in Indianapolis were out of their banks and hundreds of residences were flooded. All of the levees were threatening to be topped by the White River and Fall Creek.

1913 advertisement for the National Motor Vehicle Company of Indianapolis. These vehicles were favored during the flood by newspaper reporters to travel through flooded areas.

The Indianapolis & Vincennes Railroad Bridge is Swept Away

Indianapolis & Vincennes Railroad Bridge

Police kept people away from the Indianapolis & Vincennes railroad bridge over White River as they expected it to go down. This small bridge was located between the Oliver Avenue and Kentucky Avenue bridges. Just before 8 p.m., it was swept away.

Flooding East of the White River

Tuesday, March 25, 1913, 8 p.m.

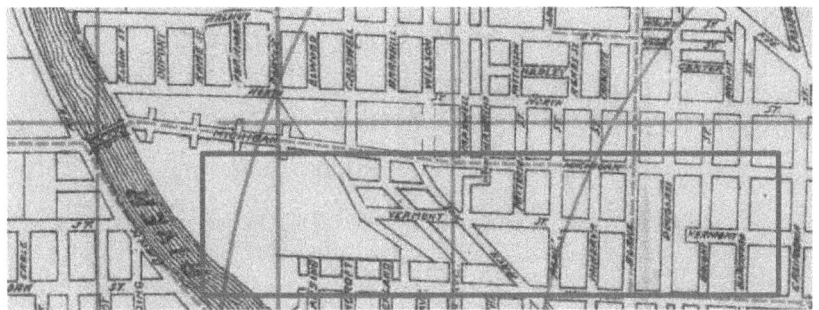

Area where citizens were rescued in blue box.

Flood scene at North and Caldwell Streets (Cornell is an error). This is on the above 1908 map.   Postcard.

By 8 p.m. Tuesday, the Indianapolis Police Department had succeeded in rescuing all persons whose homes were east of the White River, all the way to Douglass Street, laying between Michigan Street to the north and New York Street to the south.

This neighborhood was known as Cerealinetown. This comprises much of the current IUPUI college campus in 2017.

Rescue Operations on Fall Creek

IFD Captain John Monaghan

While the men of the Indianapolis Police Department were trying to warn residents

---

48   Indianapolis Firefighters Museum Collection.

on the south side of Fall Creek that their homes were in danger, four Indianapolis firemen were helping people evacuate their homes on the north side of the creek.

Fireman Robert Bruce

They were Captain John Monaghan and Firemen Springer, Statt, Fred Johnson and Robert Bruce, of Engine Company No. 14, stationed at 2960 North Kenwood Avenue. When they heard that the north bank of Fall Creek was crumbling, they took the

---

[49] Indianapolis Firefighters Museum Collection.

horses from the barn and did good work, wading into shoulder deep water to rescue endangered citizens, working into the morning.

50

Also involved in the rescue operations in this area were the men of Hose Company 16, located at 1602 Carrollton Avenue. This company had been the first African-American company of firefighters with the Indianapolis Fire Department since 1876,

---

50 Both photos from the Indianapolis Firefighters Museum Collection

The following men took their equipment several blocks north to aid the residents: Captain Clarence W. Miller, John Logan, William McGee and Claude C. Burns.

Broad Ripple under Water

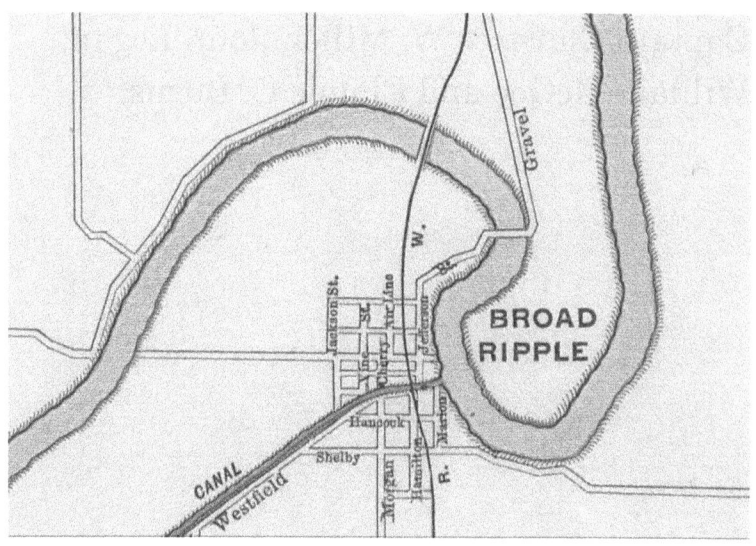

51

---

[51] *The Indianapolis News*, March 26, 1913. Indiana State Library microfilm

By nightfall, half of the town of Broad Ripple was under water, while a large number of men were desperately carrying sand bags to build up the levees near the locks of the canal to prevent the rest of the town from being flooded. These efforts were reportedly showing results.

Several small homes were overturned in the northern half. Water was six feet deep in town and was over 12 feet deep above the Broad Ripple dam.

Damage done on Bellefontaine Street, Broad Ripple. Hotel European on left. This address was named 6433 Westfield Boulevard and was the home of the Broad Ripple Pet Center in recent years.

---

[52] Damage from the 1913 Flood in Broad Ripple.
Bass Photo Co Collection, Indiana Historical Society

Evacuation Order Ignored

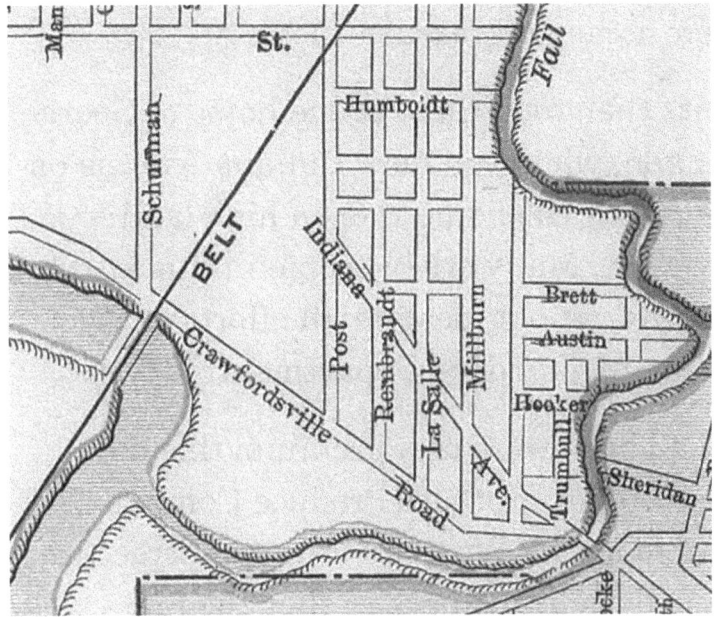

The police warned residents in the area of Indiana Avenue and Crawfordsville Road, along a levee, to evacuate. Most refused to leave, saying they would depend on the advice of experienced levee men who lived there. Several hours later, when the levee was broken in three places, they frantically called for assistance.

In the Emerichsville neighborhood on White River, Mr. & Mrs. Frank A. Vestal remained in their home too long and had to climb onto the roof. Justice of the Peace E.L. Deitz, learning of this, got in his boat and went to their home and rescued them.

Deitz then took them to the home of George Carlton, who lived near Indiana Avenue on the river. His home was on high land however. Many other people in this area couldn't get out, despite all efforts of the Indianapolis Police Department.

Telephones were at a premium this day. The Strobel Brothers Produce Company, located at 812 West Washington Street, opened their business so that the few officers on that side of town, as well as reporters, who were watching the threatened Washington Street Bridge, could use them. This allowed Captain George V. Coffin's men to report to headquarters.

473 Sandwiches to go

Tuesday, March 25, 1913, 9 p.m.

About 9 o'clock this night, volunteer Charles Rogers was working in a small boat to aid in the rescue of people just west of the Belt Railroad tracks on Washington Street. With him was Clarence Burns, 28, of 534 Miley Avenue.

Their boat was being taken from the flood zone near School No. 16. As reported by Sergeant Harry Franklin, the boat snapped in two in a strong current and Rogers went down and was carried away. He was thought drowned but this wasn't confirmed. Burns wasn't seen again that night.

After they survived their dangerous trip under the Belt Railroad overpass, Sergeant Franklin and his rescue party deemed it impossible to reach the school from Washington Street, due to the current. They went to Hose Company 18 a few blocks west, on Washington Street. There, Franklin arranged with W.E. Davis, chairman of the board of safety, and Fire Chief Coots to have the hose wagon of Hose Company 18, 1915 West Washington Street, to haul their boat to New York Street. Franklin estimated it would take 15 minutes to do this.

Captain Marion B. Kemper at Hose Company 18 agreed to this, according to Harry Franklin. Franklin went to a restaurant to requisition the food and coffee.

Franklin returned to the fire house and found that "Captain Kemper began to sidestep. He suggested that we try and hire a wagon. We called a transfer man and found he had no wagons west of the river."

CASS CONNAWAY AND BILLY TEUBNER.

The boat they used to rescue 400 people.

At this point, Teubner and Connaway "borrowed" a horse from a livery stable and stole a wagon from the Belmont Telephone Exchange to haul their boat. They were assisted by IFD Fireman Edwin J. Barnes of Hose Company 18.

Sergeant Franklin and his party launched their boat from the west side of the Washington Street Bridge and started to the relief of Captain Coffin and his 473 refugees in a school building. Franklin was frustrated, as several hours had been wasted dealing with Captain Kemper.

From William T. Riley's journal: *Eight foot of water at Engine House on Harding Street and Morris Street at 9 p.m.*

Ten Foot Surge of Water

Tuesday, March 25, 1913, 10 p.m.

While riding through the Vandalia yards on the Cincinnati, Hamilton & Dayton Railroad at 10 p.m., Conductor H.C. Tutt, saw a boy fall into the water, trying to cross a washout.

The child, later identified as 12-year old Charles Harrison of Terre Haute, cried for help. Tutt jumped into the water at Harding Street and after a lengthy struggle, both were saved after long boards were thrown to them.

After working two hours to move their furniture to the second floor of their home at 1079 River Avenue, Philander Gray and son William, 21, tried to make their way to safety at 10 p.m. They waded toward Morris Street, a block away.

The levee broke near the Morris Street Bridge about 10 p.m., sending a great surge of water into West Indianapolis. This breach raised the level of flood waters to between ten and fifteen feet, making survival in single story homes almost impossible.

Philander and William Gray were caught in this flood surge. The surge was 10-15 feet high and they grabbed the switching tower on the northeast side of the Belt Railroad tracks. They pulled themselves out of the water for an unknown amount of time.

They then decided to try to reach the railroad tracks and were swept off their feet at some point. They were separated and when the son reached safety at Harding and Morris Streets, his father Philander was not behind him. He thought he probably was rescued. This is from an account by grandson John Repass. [53]

At 10:40 p.m., the lights in the area of Morris Street and Kentucky Avenue went out, leaving only the lanterns in boats for illumination.

---

[53] http://www.westindianapolis.org/wp-content/uploads/2010/12/History-Vol-4.pdf

Father Joseph F. Weber, pastor of the Church of the Assumption on Blaine Avenue, heard cries for help coming from a home at or around 1107 Harding Street, near his rectory. "I heard cries coming from this house for several hours Tuesday night, and I am certain no rescue party reached this family," he said later.

Father Weber lived on high ground and when he heard the cries which came from low ground, he saw the water was about to reach the second story. He stood at his back fence for a long time, yelling to the man to break a hole through the plaster and climb into the attic or on the roof.

However, he could not make himself heard. He tried but failed, to make a raft to reach the family. "I think a man, wife and two or three children lived in that house and I fear they lost their lives," he said.

Two blocks north of there, rescuer William Harryman reported someone marooned in the area of River Avenue. Bunny Long heard a voice and thought it was coming from 907 River Avenue, where Mary Smith, age 76, had stayed to protect her belongings. Long tried his best to reach this house but was almost killed by a current that swept him away.

The Volunteer Boatmen

On the "hill", the highest point in West Indianapolis, men spent the night of March 25-26th building skiffs for rescue work. "The Hill", as it was known, was generally between Morris Street on the south and west of Harding Street. The "valley" was everything east to the river, a lowland which was flooded.

South of Washington Street, there were two jumping off points for the rescue boats, the Marion Motor Company's offices and the Indianapolis Abattoir Company's plant. The latter was located on Morris Street near White River. From here, boats rowed into the choppy currents and came back, sometimes loaded with refugees, sometimes empty.

54 Jack Lang (left) and Larry Dorrence.

Among the many volunteer rescuers was Larry Dorrence. Dorrence was a young man in the railroad yards on the southwest side, waiting for a train to take him home to Owensboro, Kentucky. When the flood washed this area out, Dorrence decided to volunteer his services.

For the next 48 hours, he rowed a boat, assisting with the rescues. By Saturday, Larry Dorrence was delirious as a result of his work. Father Weber took him to

---

[54] *The Indianapolis News*, April 2, 1913, p.4. Indiana State Library microfilm.

schoolhouse of his church and put him in bed.

There, another young man, Jack Lang, nursed Dorrence back to health. Lang was himself a rescuer, having worked since the flood began.

On March 26th, fifteen sailors from the U.S. Navy recruiting station in Indianapolis were offered to Superintendent Hyland by Lieutenant E.B. Armstrong, in charge. Hyland accepted the offer and the men joined the rescue efforts at 12:30 p.m. All of them had sea duty and their seamanship provided confidence and guidance among the estimated 200 men working the boats.

Joel Baker, an Indiana University student who found himself marooned on the Hill in West Indianapolis, reported that while working with rescue parties he observed 19 rowboats and one motorboat being used. He reported the bodies of two babies and three men were removed.

The Bridge Goes Down with a Roar

[55] Vandalia Railroad Bridge over White River.

Tuesday, March 25, 1913, 11 p.m.

The old Vandalia railroad bridge began being undermined by the water at 11 p.m. It was south of the new Vandalia railroad bridge. Railroad employees tried a tactic used on other railroad bridges during the Great Flood of 1913, placing ten coal cars, two of them filled with bricks, on the bridge to weigh it down. At 12:20 a.m., the bridge

---

[55] From "Twelve Views of the Indianapolis Flood of March 1913" published by C.A. Tutewiler, authors possession.

went down "with a roar" heard by persons standing at the corner of Washington and Illinois Streets.

The old Vandalia Railroad Bridge remains, above (Postcard)

The remains of the old Vandalia Railroad Bridge.

---

[56] The Indiana Album: Barbara Stevens Collection.

Right around midnight, the Taggart Baking Company announced that it would make available to relief workers an unlimited supply of bread for citizens of the western part of Indianapolis who needed food.

IPD Patrolmen Charles W. Dolan and Arthur fields, searching a young man suspected of looting homes in West Indianapolis.

---

[57] *The Indianapolis News*, March 26, 1913. Indiana State Library microfilm

Wednesday, March 26, 1913

Author's map of the approximate area flooded in 1913, on a 2018 map of Indianapolis. The area stretched from 38th Street on the north to south of Raymond Street on the south.

Early in the morning five boats were engaged in rescue work near the Kentucky Avenue Bridge, with fresh volunteers replacing those who were worn out. The currents in West Indianapolis made this work difficult and dangerous, being very swift. Women and children were taken first in the boats. Most of the rescues were made from the second story windows.

30th and Meridian Street Flooding

Meridian Street Bridge over Fall Creek wrecked. Postcard.

During the night of March 25-26th, hundreds of spectators on the north side watched as about fifty feet of Fall Creek boulevard, east of Meridian Street, crumbled away in the flood. It was followed about midnight by part of the Meridian Street Bridge collapsing into Fall Creek. Before dawn, a large portion of this concrete bridge had gone down.

Central Avenue and East 30th Street, near Fall Creek. Postcard.

Lieutenant Ira L. Leet was appointed district patrolman March 18, 1895, and promoted to sergeant June 13, 1908, and to lieutenant April 6, 1910.

58

When the Meridian Street Bridge collapsed, Lieutenant Ira Leet and a squad of policemen were sent in to wake up the residents. Police were blunt in their warnings to residents to evacuate now. They went along Capitol Avenue, warning

---

[58] 1913 IPD Yearbook, Lichtenberger History Room.

the occupants of every other house and asking them to wake up their neighbors and repeat the warning. "The boulevard levee is going down and the bridge has already crumbled. These houses may be under water in a few minutes."

They roped off the bridge and stream so that the sightseers would not be endangered and patrolled through the night. Residents were heartened when the water began receding after midnight, slowly.

Ruins of Meridian Street Bridge over Fall Creek. [59]

[60] Ruins of the Meridian Street Bridge

---

[59] From "Twelve Views of the Indianapolis Flood of March 1913" published by C.A. Tutewiler, authors possession.
[60] Engineering News Record, Vol. 69, p.873, April 24, 1913.

Snow adds to misery of victims and rescuers

61 "Snow added to misery of victims and rescuers."

Cries for Help go Silent

Wednesday, March 26, 1913, 1 a.m.

About 1 a.m., Sergeant Franklin's relief boat arrived at School No. 16. They were worn out completely and unable to pull their boat through the doors of the schoolhouse. The school was now surrounded with water 8 feet deep. There

---

[61] From "Twelve Views of the Indianapolis Flood of March 1913" published by C.A. Tutewiler, authors possession.

was a strong concern about the spread of disease in the current conditions at the school. They had to evacuate these people to better shelter. Coffin and the other officers spent the night in the school. Coffin borrowed some clothing for half frozen Cass Connaway and made him put them on.

There were 300 children in the school and while Coffin was absent, their cry of "Where is my captain?" was frequently heard. He was fond of children. In trips carrying between three and six persons, Coffin ferried them to houses on Washington Street and the Vandalia railroad tracks.

Breaking into a grocery store to get them food to eat, Coffin obtained oil stoves, provisions and blankets for people who were being cared for in churches located at Miley Avenue and West Washington Street and at New York Street and Elder Avenue.

During this night, Sergeant Harley Reed and volunteer Albert Harris made about 20 trips to people marooned in their homes.

"We saw three drowned," Reed said later. "People across the street from them yelled at us and pointed to the house. We rowed over only to see the three lying there dead and we could not reach them."

Wednesday, March 26, 1913, 1:30 a.m.

About 1:30 a.m., almost all rescue work in West Indianapolis was stopped, due to the exhaustion of the workers and poor visibility due to the heavy snow. At this time, many persons remained stranded west of White River on the roofs of their home or in the upper stories.

Cries of distress were widely reported to be heard in the early hours of the night. The boat operated by Albert Harris and Sergeant Harley Reed was the only one which returned to the east side of White River, near Morris Street.

Harris said, "I believe many are drowned over there", waving his arm toward the water-covered area. "We worked until 1:30. Then we had to tell them that we must quit.

I told them we'd come again this morning, as soon as I got a little rest."

"I don't know how many are left over there. We rescued at least eighty. The water is ten feet to fifteen feet deep in many streets of West Indianapolis. We worked until we could work no longer."

Captain A.J. Perry, commander of Company H of the Indiana National Guard, which patrolled the Oliver Avenue Bridge, reported, "Two or three boats worked until late in the night, answering the cries for help, but gradually, the cries began to grow more feeble. At about 3 o'clock we couldn't hear them anymore."

Wednesday, March 26, 1913, 4 a.m.

Chester Arnold, age 19, of 546 Alton Street, tried to swim at 4 a.m. this morning from the Peoria & Eastern Railroad tracks to the Vandalia tracks. This was near the Belt Railroad in West Indianapolis. He was trying to reach his home. The railroad grades were the only thing above water here.

A man named Charles Wells saw Arnold jump into the water and tried to save him when he saw him sink below the water. Wells reported this to Patrolman Thomas McCoy but it was too late to do anything.

In an interview with *The Indianapolis News*, Sergeant Harry Franklin said he removed several hundred people from their homes in a motor boat but a number refused to leave until the police insisted they do so. He said that few, if any people were left in West Indianapolis and was optimistic that the death toll would be low. He discounted large numbers of people drowned.

Wednesday, March 26, 1913, 5 a.m.

At 5 a.m., Sergeant Harley Reed of IPD reported that the water in West Indianapolis had receded six inches. Water still stood at 10-15 feet deep however, as far as the eye could see.

Broad Ripple Water Receding

Homes in Broad Ripple submerged.

It was reported at dawn that the water level in Broad Ripple had receded about five inches since midnight and that the immediate danger of the entire town being flooded had passed. Citizens went to work all night strengthening the levee where the river and the canal met.

Indianapolis Divided

Between 5 and 6 a.m., the West Washington Street Bridge was under a severe strain, its girders being struck by tons of debris. Two large houses had rammed into the west end of it. The floor had been slowly crumbling in the early morning hours of Wednesday, March 26th.

Out for a morning drive to road test a car for the Cole Motor Company was Fred "Red" Barnett. He drove west on Michigan Street across the White River, then went south five blocks to Washington Street and turned left, to head back toward town. Ahead was the Washington Street Bridge.

As he passed by the street car barns west of the river, he noticed the water was up to the hubs of the car. He had to cross a small wooden bridge a block from the river first. The test car started to slide a bit as he crossed.

As he drove onto it, the bridge started to shake, which scared Barnett. He put the car into reverse and backed off the bridge. He had only gone a quarter of a block when the bridge fell into the White River with a tremendous crash and resulting splash. He sat there and shivered with fear.

This was just before 6 a.m. Wednesday when the east span fell into the White River. The east end of the bridge tore loose from the pier, the road bed sinking beneath the water. High tension wires which were bringing electricity for the Indianapolis Street Railway Company were almost at water level. The honor of being the "last man to get off the bridge" belonged to Patrolman Arthur Duffy or rescuer Lemuel Christie, who both claimed the title.

The middle span of the bridge also crashed into the river. As the rest of the bridge fell, it took out the telephone and telegraph cables, rupturing service and communication.

Collapse of the Washington Street Bridge

[62] West Washington Street Bridge One Hour Before It Collapsed, March 1913. Indiana Historical Society, P0326

This shows the Washington Street Bridge in the process of sinking into the White River.

---

[63] West Washington Street Bridge Photographed as It Fell, March 1913. Indiana Historical Society, P0326

64

---

[64] *The Indianapolis Star*, March 27, 1913. Indiana State Library microfilm

Ruins of Washington Street Bridge.

---

[65] Engineering News Record, Vol. 69, p.871, April 24, 1913.

The Washington Street Bridge after collapse, east end, looking south.

The Washington Street Bridge on March 26, 1913, west end, looking south. Postcard.

66 Bridge over West Washington Street
"swept away by the seething waters."

[66] From "Twelve Views of the Indianapolis Flood of March 1913" published by C.A. Tutewiler, authors possession.

Wednesday, March 26, 1913, 6 a.m.

[67] Washout of retaining wall and embankment along Boulevard on Fall Creek.

At daylight on March 26th, Fall Creek's bank was eroding between Meridian and Pennsylvania Streets. One hundred feet of Fall Creek Boulevard was washed out. Indianapolis patrolmen began waking residents up. Soon, most of the homes in a four block radius were evacuated.

By this time, the sections of Indianapolis that were under water included:

- Large part of West Indianapolis and territory lying to the north and extending above Washington Street.
- West Indianapolis extends from the bridges southwestward to the Morris

---

[67] Engineering News Record, Vol. 69, p.871, April 24, 1913.

Street Christian Church at Blaine Avenue and Morris Street (six blocks). In some places the water was 10-15 feet deep.
- Large territory along Fall Creek in northwest Indianapolis.
- Parts of the North Side, between Meridian Street and Fall Creek.
- Lowlands along Eagle Creek and low territory at various points along Pleasant and Pogue's Runs.

Men are using horses to move street cars from the flood zone on Michigan Street.

---

[68] Cars Caught in Flood March 1913, Indianapolis, Ind. Indiana Historical Society, P0391

At dawn, the rescuers in West Indianapolis resumed their work, which they had abandoned at 1:30 a.m. At the edge of the flood zone, men began building skiffs and scows using 2x4's, lined with tar paper.

Among these men was William T. Riley, railroad conductor. He noted in his daily journal March 26th: "We made a boat at Baumhofer's."

[69]

Harry Baumhofer with wife and daughters Janet and Nancy.

---

[69] Photo courtesy of Nancy J. Netter, great-granddaughter of Harry.

Harry J. Baumhofer, house carpenter, lived at 1740 West Morris Street, next door. The two men were brothers-in-law, having married sisters Olive and Velma Terry. They lived just out of the flood zone on "the hill."

By March 26th, there were an estimated 8,000 homeless persons living between Tenth Street and Washington Street on White River. At Michigan Street (halfway point between 10th Street and Washington Street) the water was a half-mile wide on the *east* side. Most of the bridges were still standing but water had scoured out the approaches, making crossing impossible.

The weather forecast for March 26th was colder temperatures and either rain or snow. The temperature at 7 a.m. today was 34 degrees. While rain had stopped the previous night in the northern part of Indiana, it was hoped that colder temperatures would prevent more rainfall in Indianapolis. Water levels were dropping throughout Indianapolis now, but not very much on the White River.

Belt Railroad tracks washed out south of Indianapolis. [70]

It was reported that the tracks of the Belt Railroad, which were elevated, were washed away, from the Kentucky Avenue shops to the White River. Mr. J.J. Liddy, superintendent of the Belt Railroad, took a gang of men on switch engines and tried to reach five engines near the Union stockyards. The tracks were washed out, running as deep into the floodwaters as he could.

This took them to the section of West Indianapolis which was on the southwest edge of the flood zone. Suddenly, the men heard the cries of distressed victims of the flood. "There was nothing we could do – water from ten to thirty feet in depth

---

[70] Engineering News Record, Vol. 69, p.873, April 24, 1913.

stretched between us and the nearest houses", said Mr. Liddy.

"Women and children were screaming and men were shouting for help. Revolver shots broke out now and then. I believe there were many drowned in this section of West Indianapolis."

Wednesday, March 26, 1913, 7 a.m.

From William T. Riley's journal: *March 26. Big Flood. Cold rain. Snowed heavy flakes and thundered*[71] *while it snowed. We made a boat at Baumhofer's. The water run 2 foot over Morris Street and Belt Railway 7 a.m.*

By this time Wednesday, railroad traffic into Indianapolis was at a total standstill. Telephone and telegraph service to the city was also cut off. The latest train arriving in what was then known as "The Crossroads of America" due to the conjunction of so many railroads, arrived from Chicago at 3:20 p.m. Tuesday. This disruption of traffic and communication was also due to the flood

---

[71] Thunder during a snow storm is a rare metrological event and is now referred to as "thundersnow."

being catastrophic in Ohio and other areas of the Midwest.

Rescue operations on March 26, 1913.

---

[72] *The Indianapolis Star*, March 27, 1913. Indiana State Library microfilm

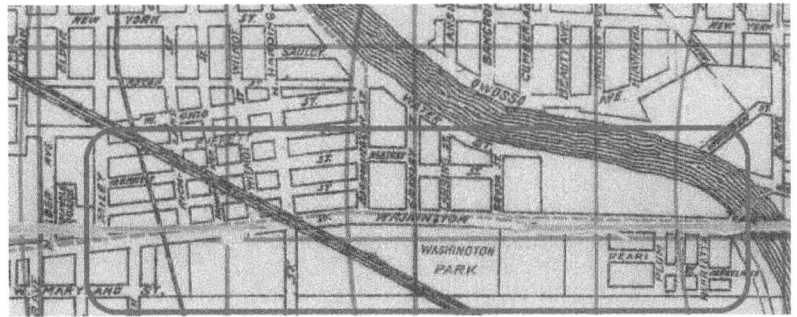

Extent of the flood to the west. Washington Park was the home of the Indianapolis baseball team.

The crest of the flood here was reached at 7 a.m. and water began falling steadily throughout Indianapolis. This was a slow process however, because of all of the massive amounts of flood water that was pouring back into the streams.

At the time of the crest of floodwaters, they reached Miley Avenue on Washington Street and didn't recede for 24-hours. The waters of Eagle Creek on the west, met the waters of White River from the east, at Belmont Avenue and the Vandalia railroad tracks.

Mr. J.G. Collicott, superintendent of the Indianapolis Public Schools, announced the suspension of all schools for the rest of the week. The main reason was the lack of water at the schools. Many were inaccessible due to the flood.

73 School Number 16

In the morning, Captain George V. Coffin and Sergeant Harry Franklin began the process of evacuating the 473 refugees from School No. 16 at 1402 West Market Street. They loaded them onto boats in groups of between three and six and took them to houses between Washington Street and the

---

[73] Public School no. 16, Oscar S. Deitch, 1923, Bass Photo Co Collection, Indiana Historical Society

Vandalia railroad tracks. One boat was manned by William R. Harriman, clerk of the Superior Court and Mr. S.S. Long, a railroad man. The trip was more than a mile long. Other officers assisting were James Black, Victor Houston and John V. Hostetler.

The last person to leave the school was Dr. O.S. Deitch. (School No. 16 was also known as the Oscar S. Deitch School). He stood in water almost covering his body for a long time, probably while waiting his turn.

He became mentally disabled, becoming violent and having to be restrained. He was taken to the home of friends at the corner of Washington Street and Miley Avenue, where he was recovering on Friday.

A Dangerous Task

Skill With Oars Useful
In Rescuing Sufferers

74

Frank Hulse (above) was lauded as one of the heroes of the flood. Starting Tuesday,

---

[74] The Indianapolis News, March 26, 1913. Indiana State Library microfilm

he worked 24-hours at the oars. He told of hearing pitiful cries during the night.

Looking southeast from Coffey Street and the Vandalia tracks.

---

[75] *The Indianapolis News*, March 26, 1913. Indiana State Library microfilm

Harry Bly

The first accident Wednesday on this part of the river among the rescuers occurred when the Reverend O.K. Downey, pastor of the Morris Street Christian Church and Harry Bly, who had been attempting to get flood victims out before the Oliver Avenue levee broke, capsized in the swift current at Oliver Avenue and Drover Street.

They had been attempting to rescue a man holding onto a telegraph pole. They were

---

[76] The Indianapolis News, April 2, 1913, p.4. Indiana State Library microfilm.

exhausted from their labors. They managed to hold onto telephone poles for 15-minutes.

As their boat was swept into Drover Street, Frank Hulse saw their predicament, jumped into his boat and started after them. They were headed toward the White River. He caught up with them and got the young man, Bly, into the boat. He then got Rev. Downey in the boat after some effort.

His boat was swept for three blocks before he got it under control and back onto Oliver Avenue. Hulse was considered the most skilled boatman working as a rescue worker. When landed, Rev. Downey fell against a nearby wall from exhaustion.

Bly, taken to a warm office, changed into dry clothing and went back to work. He was one of the most foremost rescuers, always coming back with a full boat.

77

Victor Houston   John Hostetler

There were only a few actual Indianapolis police officers on the west side of the White River to support Captain Coffin. Two of them were Patrolmen Victor Houston and John V. Hostetler. They worked tirelessly doing rescue work in the boats. At one point their boat capsized, both being thrown in the water, each holding a child.

Hostetler nearly drowned before he and the child were rescued. He collapsed from

---

[77] Lichtenberger History Room.

exhaustion. He later put on an apron to wash dishes in the Wesley Chapel.

Edgar E. Hobbs   Jerry Doody

Two other officers were Patrolmen E.E. Hobbs and Jerry Doody. They did outstanding rescue work, despite losing their homes in the flood. Both refused to be relieved until ordered to return to their homes by their superiors.

Bicycleman Thomas O'Brien, a diminutive Irishman, worked closely with Captain Coffin and Sergeant Franklin during the flood. After the flood, O'Brien's wife, who knew Captain Coffin, was one of the first into the flood zone. She hadn't heard from

---

[78] Lichtenberger History Room.

her husband for days but said she was never worried because as she told Coffin, "Captain, I knew he was with you and was safe."

Another story recounted of a rescue south of Washington Street described a boat with two police officers in it, rowing up to a house where two brothers stood on the roof, exhausted from being there for hours. They got in the boat, which began spinning in a whirlpool, capsizing.

All four were thrown in the water. The officers were able to save one brother, but the other was struggling weakly and sank out of sight. It was impossible to recover his body.

At some point Wednesday, a man was helping take flood victims out at West New York Street. He asked a man who he had rescued to pay him $2. The survivor had no money, so a companion produced the $2. As the boatman reached out for the money, a police officer standing nearby, struck him in the jaw and knocked him into the water.

The great majority of people working during this crisis did it for nothing. Mr. Lorian C. Arnold, 21, of 276 Miley Avenue on the edge of the flood in the Stringtown neighborhood and his friend Mr. Nicholson had a canoe stored in a barn at New York Street and Richland Avenue. They got their canoe out and rescued a large number of marooned people.

The Female Relief Workers

One of the women who showed heroism during this disaster was Miss Ethel Trotcky, 26, who lived on the west side. All day and all night Wednesday she aided in the rescue work at one of the landings when victims were taken from the water.

Ethel Trotcky was the daughter of Solomon Trotcky and his wife Mary Steinberg. They were Jewish immigrants from Kiev, Russia. Their other daughters were Myrtle and Jennie, who also worked very hard to relieve the suffering of the flood victims.

The Trotcky home served as headquarters for the relief workers. Solomon, who owned a clothing and shoe store, would donate a large amount of supplies to the needy.

For the first few days of the flood, women cooked for almost 100 people at this home, but it became too much for them. Sergeant Harry Franklin found two men he had known for years, Bucky Steve and Jim Hicks, African-American cooks. They took over the cooking duties and became local heroes of those in charge of the relief efforts.

Women collected a mountain of clothing for flood refugees at Tomlinson Hall. Miss Ethel Conklin was helping the Volunteers of America care for 250 people housed at the German Lutheran Church, 34 West Ohio Street. She took up a collection of $60 for use in furnishing supplies to them.

Misses Conklin, Lillian Earp and Ada Catterlin, who lived at 201 Roberts Annex, took 12 of the young children living at the church to their home for supper on Wednesday and breakfast Thursday.

One of Captain Coffin's volunteer policemen, William Harryman, clerk in

Judge Orbison's Superior Court, brought news that the persons west of the flood zone, near Belmont Avenue, were without bread, but that a baker who lived there would bake all the bread necessary if he had yeast.

An appeal was made to the General Relief Committee, and a large quantity of yeast was sent to the Oliver Street landing. Harryman then took it by boat to the baker.

Care of Refugees at Tomlinson Hall

The main refugee center in downtown Indianapolis was Tomlinson Hall, which was next to the City Market and across the Street from the Marion County Court House. Many refugees, wet and hungry, were brought directly from rescue boats to this building. The National Guard set up here but most of the aid was given by ordinary citizens, who came from all areas of Indianapolis to help.

Many of the victims were grief stricken and in a state of hysteria. It was considered very important to register incoming refugees as soon as they entered the building, so that relatives and friends looking for them could know they were safe.

Mrs. Lewis Shank, wife of the mayor and numerous other leading women from the city were here, serving food, washing dishes and doing all they could to make survivors comfortable. The food came in from bakeries, department stores and people operating food stands at the nearby City Market. "Society women" of Indianapolis were serving as waitresses.

One scene made several people turn around in tears. A little boy approached a woman at the food table and asked for a drink. There was no cold water in the hall to give him, only coffee.

Elsewhere, private citizens were throwing their homes open to homeless people and announcing that their wells were available to anyone needing water.

C. L. WEAVER,
Sergeant of Police.

[79]

Cletus L. Weaver, who was a desk sergeant at police headquarters, talked to his brother Robert this morning. Robert was a watchman at the Martin Forge Company, 510 South Harding Street. He said they were out of fuel and the building was cold, but they were safe.

---

[79] 1913 IPD Yearbook, Lichtenberger History Room.

Sergeant Weaver set off to find his brother, a journey that took five hours before he reached the plant, only to find it empty this afternoon. He hadn't received any word from his brother by the end of the day, but felt he was safe.

One Rescuer's Story

During the morning, Glenn Wells, of 537 East New York Street was in his words, "loafing" the near the Parry Manufacturing Company, observing the rescue work being done. A man came in with a canoe and asked to be relieved. A man named "Bud" and Wells volunteered to take the boat.

"During the morning, we were able to carry about ten persons from their homes to places of safety, but a stroke of bad luck stopped our work. We were paddling in the neighborhood of Warren Avenue and Harding Street when suddenly a man on a veranda roof, whom we did not see, jumped into our canoe, upsetting us. All three of us managed to catch the roof and to hold on until another boat picked us up and took us in.

"I went home and changed clothes and about 3 o'clock started out again, this time from the Oliver Avenue Bridge. On our first trip, we found a woman with three children, 4, 12 and 15 years old, in a two-story building on Division Street, near Morris. We threw a rope up to them and they fastened it and slid down into our canoe and we took them in.

"All four of them seemed to be in good spirits, although they had had nothing to eat since the levee at Morris Street broke yesterday. We then went way down in the flood district and somewhere near River Avenue and Coffey Street we found a woman lying dead with her dead babe in her arms. The water nearly filled the room and the woman was lying on a mattress stretched across a bureau and dresser top or bedposts or something like that. They were partly under water. The woman seemed to be about 30-years old and the child about a year. I never cried so hard in my life as when I saw them.

"We tried to get them out by breaking the window and reaching them with driftwood, but could not and had to give up. We then went over to Belmont Street and there we saw a man floating in the water. We could just see a part of his head and couldn't tell what he looked like.

"Both of us were exhausted and it had started to snow, so we went back to get someone to take the boat. We also were pretty sick of the job after seeing those dead people.

"No one wanted to take the boat, so we started out again. We picked up two stray boats and towed them in and then went west on Oliver to the Belt Railroad. We lifted our canoe over and then went up to the Pennsylvania tracks and lifted our boat over that.

"As we passed the plant of the Lauter Company we could see that there was about 20 feet of water in it. We went up to

Washington Street and looked west and could see the water stretching out almost to the Insane Asylum. From what we could see the asylum is in no danger from the water.

"We went back on Washington Street to Bloomington and tried to go up to the schoolhouse, (School no. 16) but the current was too swift for us and we had to go back. We started in the work in West Indianapolis again and took off a load of three women and another of three men, all of whom were in the same house.

"We saw an old couple in a house, but couldn't get to them in our boat and had to send for a flatboat that took them to the bridge. One man tried to make us take a trunk in with him and we couldn't argue with him, so left him and let another boat take him too. By that time it was dark, so we pulled our boat in and quit." (*The Indianapolis Star*, March 27, 1913)

Wednesday, March 26, 1913, 9 a.m.

JESSE M. STREIT,
Sergeant of Police.

[80]

Sergeant Jesse Streit and some volunteers took two boats, a canoe and a flat-bottomed boat, which Streit was in command of, to flooded Morris Street on March 26th. There were dozens of families imprisoned within flooded homes, within 100 yards of

---

[80] 1913 IPD Yearbook, Lichtenberger History Room.

the high ground. They shouted constantly for help, but the men on shore were helpless.

Police motor boat in Morris Street. [81]

Streit and his men braved a "treacherous" current, repeatedly to bring out a few survivors. His bravery and devotion to duty was noted by observers.

There were fifteen men stranded at the Frank Hilgemeier packing house, at

---

[81] From "Twelve Views of the Indianapolis Flood of March 1913" published by C.A. Tutewiler, authors possession.

Raymond Street and White River on Wednesday. They fired off skyrockets as a distress signal, which was seen by police in boats. Two boats went to their aid immediately. The men had been yelling in vain for hours but nobody could hear them. Then they found a dozen skyrockets in an office, left over from a July 4th celebration.

Thomas McCoy   Guy Harper

Patrolman Thomas W. McCoy, 35, found himself working in the West Indianapolis area with Patrolman Guy Harper. McCoy was a veteran of the Spanish-American war, serving as a Sergeant in the 1st Infantry Division. He saw action at the Battles of Santiago and San Juan Hill, July 1st and 3rd, in 1898.

In 1900, his regiment was sent to the Philippine Islands to fight in the guerilla war there. When he was discharged in 1902, he came to Indianapolis and joined the police department.

A timely rescue was made by Patrolmen Guy Harper and Thomas McCoy on March 26th at 918 West Pearl Street. They found Mrs. Nancy Rayno standing on her toes in the kitchen, holding onto a curtain rod to keep her head above water.

They carried her to a boat and later to an ambulance. She was taken to a hospital in poor condition, where she celebrated her 100th birthday on March 27th.

The City Mobilizes

Wednesday, March 26, 1913, 10 a.m.

At 10 a.m., the first meeting of a hastily organized General Relief Committee sat down in Mayor Lew Shank's office in City Hall. It was headed by William J. Mooney as chairman.

Other members of the committee were: S.A. Fletcher, treasurer, F.D. Loomis, secretary, J.H. Holliday, E.C. Atkins, Rev. F.S.C. Wicks, George Vonnegut, F.M. Ayres, J.W. Lilly, Hilton U. Brown, Ernest Bross, Rev. F.M. Feuerlicht, C.J. Lynn, Joseph B. Kealing, Joseph C. Schaf, R.O. Hawkins, Frank Duffy, Ida V. Jontz, Hazel Verry, H.B. Gates, Louis Hollweg, Samuel E. Rauh, George F. Kirkhoff and C. S. Grout.

The committee took up the many issues such as the clothing and feeding of refugees who were being housed at Tomlinson Hall, around the corner.

One of their immediate decisions was to name a committee on food, fuel and clothing, which made sandwiches and hot coffee available to 200 refugees at Tomlinson Hall within a short time. Manual High School on the south side was designated as a shelter for 278 refugees. The school was in the charge of Captain Frank Foxworthy of the National Guard Hospital Corps, and Dr. Jane Ketcham and Dr. E. Russell Bush, health inspectors.

The committee called upon Governor Ralston to detail Captain P.A. Davis of the Quartermaster General's staff of the Indiana National Guard. His military experience would bring efficiency to the distribution of warm food, bedding and shelter.

There had been complaints on Wednesday that there wasn't anybody in charge of the men operating the boats doing the rescue work. The general relief committee put General Vonnegut in charge of a subcommittee, to manage the landings with persons having authority.

Other subcommittees were formed for these areas with designated heads:

- Finance (F.M. Ayres)
- Housing (George Vonnegut)
- Food, Fuel and Clothing (R.O. Hawkins)
- Finance (S.A. Fletcher)

There was a moment during this meeting in Mayor Shank's office when a call came in from the office of the mayor of Dayton, Ohio. His voice could barely be heard. Annis Burk, Mayor Shank's secretary, who took the call, asked everybody in the room to be still.

"Help! Help! For God's sake send us help. Half of the town is submerged and the other half is burning."

The voice was then silenced and the call ended. The committee discussed the possibility of sending relief to Dayton, which suffered a heavy loss of life in this catastrophe. However, there was no way to send aid due to transportation being disrupted at that time.

Oliver Avenue Levee Breaks

[82] View looking south from the west end of the Oliver Avenue Bridge, where another levee broke.

Wednesday, March 26, 1913, 10:30 a.m.

At 10:30 a.m. Wednesday, another disastrous levee break occurred. The wall on the west side of the White River, 300 feet south of the Oliver Avenue Bridge, gave

---

[82] Puritan Bed Spring Company, from Oliver Avenue Bridge, flood damage, 1913, Bass Photo Co Collection, Indiana Historical Society

way. Men working throughout the previous night had built it up two additional feet. At first it was about ten feet wide, slowly raising the water level in West Indianapolis by another two feet over many streets in the neighborhood. It also increased the number of unpredictable currents flowing through these streets.

Following this levee collapse, the Indianapolis Police Department opened up a new place to do their rescue work, near the Indianapolis Abattoir Company, wholesale butchers located on Morris Street near the White River.

The elevated ground it was located on was now an island and a port from which IPD could launch their boats and go into West Indianapolis.

At the Church of the Assumption, 1117 Blaine Avenue, which had 200 survivors housed there, they found water reaching the church after the Oliver Avenue levee broke at 10:30 a.m. The people had to be evacuated again.

Some of the residents who were reached by rescue boats said they were fine where they were except for a shortage of food and declined rescue. These people were left ready to eat food provided by the Abattoir Company.

Mr. J.J. Liddy, superintendent of the Belt Railroad, took a switch engine and coach, around the Belt, from Rural Street on the east side of Indianapolis, west to the Piel Brothers Starch works, where 500 feet of track had been washed out.

CHAS. METCALFE,
Sergeant of Police.

83

They had loaded a boat on the train which was then unloaded, in order to reach 15 small homes on the west side of Bridge Street, that were in water up to the second floor.

Liddy and his party found that the residents refused to leave. Sergeant

---

[83] 1913 IPD Yearbook, Lichtenberger History Room.

Charles Metcalfe of IPD, who had a larger police boat, also reached the homes but they refused to leave. He then brought them meat from the Abattoir Company.

MOTHER AND CHILDREN SAFE

Mrs. Jessie Zehr and children, who were rescued from 1062 West McCarty Street by patrolman Bert Atkins (in stern of boat) and an assistant who said he was "too busy to give his name." The picture was taken as they approached the Oliver Avenue Bridge in West Indianapolis.
The Indianapolis News – March 26, 1913

Among the rescues was that of Mrs. Jessie Zehr, Mrs. Louise Scalf and thirteen children, from their home at 1062 West

McCarty Street the morning of March 26th. The home was on higher ground and was a place of refuge for the neighbors. Mrs. Scalf's husband and five sons were left behind (women and children first was the rule during this catastrophe). She had tears in her eyes, pleading with the boatmen to go back for them, saying they were starving and had no water.

Patrolman Bert Atkins in rear of boat on Oliver Avenue. This was placed in his personnel file as testament to his place on the "Flood Roll of Honor."[84]

---

[84] Lichtenberger History Room.

Rescue operations on March 26, 1913 on Oliver Avenue. Policeman in rear of boat. [85]

About six rowboats worked along Oliver Avenue, which had fairly calm waters to work in, except where other streets intersected it. About 100 people were rescued after day break from their homes on March 26th.

---

[85] *The Indianapolis Star*, March 27, 1913. Indiana State Library microfilm

People needing medical care were taken to the Marion Motor Company's plant nearby, which housed a temporary hospital. Ambulances took people from there to regular hospitals.

There were stories told by the refugees of hearing cries for help from people in streets that were on lower ground. The screams were that they would be drowned in a short time.

Mr. L.C. Huddleston, who was a member of a rescue party working in west Morris Street, reported he saw the bodies of a man, a woman and two children in the first house east of the Belt Railroad. He couldn't identify them. They had apparently been caught in a small house and forced against the ceiling by the high water.

A Snowstorm Strikes Indianapolis

Wednesday, March 26, 1913, 12 p.m.

At noon, a blinding snowstorm passed through Indianapolis, causing several serious traffic accidents downtown. Two people were struck by autos at the corner of New York Street and Massachusetts Avenue.

Another man was struck crossing the street at Massachusetts Avenue and Delaware Street. While a crowd gathered here, a man drove up on Delaware Street and struck 15-year old Earl Fitchett, knocking him down. Traffic Officer Kerins blamed automobile drivers for taking advantage of the traffic officers since street car service ended.

There were a lot of complaints this day about selfish people who owned a car not offering rides to people walking and worse, seemed to enjoy seeing others walk while they drove.

During this disaster, some taxi drivers charged from a nickel to a quarter for a ride. However, an ice company sent its wagons downtown and ordered the drivers to give workers rides home for free. A large express company did the same thing.

Indianapolis temperature fell slightly below freezing in the afternoon, increasing the suffering for people in the flood zones.

This afternoon, Superintendent of Police Hyland sent 1,000 loaves of bread across the White River at Morris Street by motor boat. The trip was aborted however because the current was too strong.

The Tragedy of Mary Smith

Wednesday afternoon, Mr. Lawrence Fanning of 909 River Avenue, whose wife Ella had fled Tuesday, heard a voice coming from 907 River Avenue where Mrs. Mary Smith had decided to wait out the flood.

---

[86] *The Indianapolis Star*, April 1, 1913. Indiana State Library microfilm.

He tried to paddle a boat to her house but was blocked by debris.

Othello Thomas   William E. Row

Not long afterward, IPD Mounted Patrolmen Grosset and Othello Thomas, led by Sergeant William E. Row, were directed to Mrs. Smith's home by Lt. Barmfuhrer. There, they found her body, lying across the footboard of the bed, face down.

From the mark of the water level of the interior of the home, it would have reached chin level. They felt she had stood on her bed for 18 hours, holding her chin above the water line, before collapsing from exhaustion and drowning, about 9 p.m.

Savior of the Animals

Patrolman Oscar A. Merrill

During Wednesday, the police departments' Humane Officer, Patrolman Oscar Merrill, along with Mr. William E. Reiley, attorney, had spent 50-60 hours without sleep, operating a rowboat in West Indianapolis.

On this date, paddling in the back waters of the Oliver Avenue bridge, they found two horses that had taken refuge on the porch of a dwelling.

Reiley got on the porch and hitched the horses to a makeshift halter, and with

Merrill's assistance, brought the horses to dry land. After rescuing a family which had been forced to take refuge in the attic of a home on Oliver Avenue, Reiley and Merrill returned there and took a small spaniel from the woodshed where it was marooned on some floating lumber.

When an effort was made to put the animal in one of the stalls at the pound, it refused to leave its rescuer.

Merrill, a dog lover, found two just as the bigger one was about to drown while swimming in water three feet deep inside a home. The smaller one was on a bed. He rescued both. These and other dogs as well as chickens, were rescued and taken to the dog pound to await their owners.

87 Kingan & Company Bridge nearly collapsed.

---

87 The Indiana Album: Barbara Stevens Collection.

Boatman Howard Foster found a beautiful black horse on a porch on Birch Street this afternoon. While getting the horse off the porch, his boat went under the water. The horse swam several blocks while one of the rescuers held his head above water and another paddled the canoe. The horse was taken to the Dog Pound.

The wreck of the Washington Street Bridge appeared on many Postcards. Looking west. Postcard.

There were various estimates of the dead by mid-day on Wednesday, ranging from 20 to 200 but no one would be able to get a good total until the water went down in West Indianapolis.

Feeding the Flood Sufferers

FLOUR FOR HUNGRY HAUGHVILLE.

On the afternoon of March 26th, Sergeant Harley Reed made his way to the location of Captain Coffin and Sergeant Franklin in

---

[88] *The Indianapolis News*, March 29, 1913. Indiana State Library microfilm

Haughville, north of the flooded area of "West Indianapolis."

Reed had obtained 100 loaves of bread from the County Poor Farm and Central State Insane Hospital. This bread and other food was prepared there by IPD Patrolman Leonard B. Forsythe. Sgt. Reed and Patrolman Cox reported that the situation was "well in hand" in west Indianapolis. All persons known to be in danger had been rescued.

This afternoon, Captain Coffin went to the Mt. Jackson neighborhood of Indianapolis to get provisions. Mt. Jackson, known in 2017 as the Hawthorne neighborhood, was a settlement farther west, bounded on the south by Washington Street, on the west by Tibbs Avenue, on the north by Michigan Street, and on the east by Belmont Avenue. It was out of the flood zone.

"More Powerful than the Rapids of the Yukon"

Late in the afternoon, volunteer rescuer John S. Taggart, of the Archey-Atkins Company, got in a canoe at the Oliver Avenue Bridge, starting toward the southwest. He heard a lot of gunfire and heard about ten people pleading for help. They hadn't eaten in two days.

He was unable to stop to help due to the fast current at near the Nordyke & Marmon Company's plant at Kentucky Avenue and Morris Street.

He was then swept past the Indianapolis Abattoir Company's plant before he realized that he himself was in serious trouble. He yelled for help and men at the plant threw him a line.

He later said that nothing but a powerful motor boat could handle the fast current of the White River, which he described as "more powerful than the rapids of the Yukon in Alaska." That's why he volunteered, he had experience in a canoe on the Yukon.

He observed there were 25 men stranded at the Nordyke & Marmon plant, on the second floor. There were also men hanging from trees, asking for help, who had also started out as rescuers.

Strange Scenes in West Indianapolis

Wednesday, March 26, 1913, 6 p.m.

The rescue work in West Indianapolis continued into the night, the only light being provided by 20 Prest-O-Light tanks and motorcycle lanterns, furnished to the relief committee by Indianapolis 500 co-founder Carl Fisher's Prest-O-Light plant. Company secretary-treasurer James A. Allison (also a co-founder) also provided tanks and a search light for the roof of the Marion Automobile Company.

The previous night, there was no light except for lanterns and the light from automobile headlights pointed toward the flood zone from dry land.

The water near Oliver Avenue was placid enough to do rescue work, but the force of the torrent increased as they went south of the bridge. Three hundred yards south of the bridge, the White River had split into two forks, the new offshoot going to the southwest being described as a "veritable death trap" to families that hadn't yet been reached and also to the rescuers risking their lives.

There were many scenes of victims being taken from the boats by men wading in hip deep water. One elderly woman reprimanded a police officer trying to lift her out of the boat.

"Indeed, I can get out myself," she shouted. "I want you to know that I am 76 years old, that I have seen and passed through all kinds of trouble and that I am able to take care of myself." The policeman stepped back, showing admiration at the woman's spunk.

One rescue that came Wednesday was of Mrs. Mary Pryor and her two young sons, at 1106 River Avenue. They were in need of medical treatment from exposure and were rushed to the hospital.

When the Morris Street levee broke, the waters rushed toward her home and caught them before they could leave. The three of them spent the night in the second floor of their home.

When police arrived at a home on Oliver Avenue in which a number of people were crowded in a small attic, the people refused to leave. They were carrying on a religious service, paying no attention to the police commands. Finally, a patrolman ordered several of the women to leave, which they did. A man refused to leave or accept any food or water.

Another family of five was rescued this night, but refused to get into the boat unless the family dog was also taken. The mother said "Leave that dog? Indeed, you won't. That dog has stuck with us for 18 years and we are going to stick with him now." The dog was the first to enter the boat and happily lay down in the bottom of it.

As rescuers plied their way through the darkened streets, they were startled to hear someone playing ragtime music on a piano. They rowed to a two-story building and saw a family standing on the second floor around a piano. A young woman was playing. The group was rescued and were cheerful when they landed at the Oliver Avenue Bridge.

On Coffey Street, just south of Oliver Avenue this date a man on top of the roof of his home was asked how long he expected to stay and he yelled, "The whole night long." His two-story home was covered with water up over the first-floor windows. Inside a player piano was playing and five people were holding a "wet party" inside. Children were singing.

Another report came from an Oliver Avenue boatman that a man was singing *"When I get you alone tonight"* from a second story window. Still another man, described as elderly, was playing his violin in a house half submerged. He refused to be rescued.

There were a lot of saloons in this district and while some people thought it saved a lot of the lives of the refugees crowded in them, the police asserted it caused as many to be lost. One such case was that of Roy Lane, charged with drunkenness. Before Judge Collins in Police Court on Wednesday, Lane admitted that he was intoxicated, but said he had overindulged in stimulants to ward off the cold while working to rescue some of the flood victims the night before, after escaping from his own home. Judge Collins said, "I'm kind-a with these flood sufferers," as he let Lane and other survivors off with an $11 fine.

About 50 of these survivors were rescued by the men of Indianapolis Fire Department Station House No. 19 in West Indianapolis, whose station was flooded but they continued protecting citizens. These firefighters were John Monahan, J.E. Zenor, M.C. Dickson, F.M. Quinn and C.F. Leser.

One of their rescues involved Fireman John Monahan. He heard an old man named Ben Gammin, who lived in a box car, crying for help. He lived near Ray Street and the river. Rescuers heard the cries.

The currents in this area made this a dangerous trip, but Monahan volunteered to go. His canoe was carried three blocks off course but he managed to get to the box car. When he did, Ben Gammin was up to his chin in water. Monahan rescued him.

These people were taken to School No. 49, at Morris and Kappes Streets on Wednesday. They were described as being well and happy, with sufficient provisions on hand, but they did need drinking water.

The Danger of Looting Looms

At police headquarters in Indianapolis, Captain William Holtz stated that he was expecting an epidemic of looting and other crimes to follow when the water receded.

---

[89] 1913 IPD Yearbook, Lichtenberger History Room.

He based this on what had happened in other cities.

"As soon as the water recedes to allow a man to walk through the flooded districts, the looting will begin. We are looking for it in every way. As a warning to the flood victims, let me say that they should waste no time in returning to homes so hurriedly deserted."

That night, Captain Holtz, William E. Davis, chairman of the Board of Safety and Superintendent Martin Hyland left headquarters in a patrol wagon. They took coffee and sandwiches to policemen and soldiers on guard duty in each flood district. The men ate and drank all they could. They had been suffering due to the strain, snow and cold.

Coffin Orders the Saloons Closed

Wednesday, March 26, 1913, 8 p.m.

Captain Coffin noticed there was too much drinking going on by Wednesday evening and he ordered the saloons ordered closed at

8 p.m. If they weren't, the liquor would be poured out into the streets. It isn't politically correct by today's standards, but since there was no jail available, the most offensive drunks showing no regard for the rights of others was administered a severe beating by the police, as an example to others.

Wednesday night, Dan Healy was going down West Washington Street in a motor boat but it threw him out at the P. & E. railroad tracks. Luckily, four men who had just arrived from Crawfordsville, pulled him out with a rope into their motor boat. They were Noble Dean, Burt McDaniel, Otis and Cecil Faust.

Most of the boatmen working from the Oliver Avenue landing quit for the night by 8 p.m. On the west side of the flood zone, on "The Hill", residents worked all night, rescuing their neighbors to the east in "The Valley."

As night came and snow was falling, there was greater emphasis on rescuing the few people believed to be in the flooded area, fearing they might not survive the night. A large bonfire was lit in Morris Street at the water's edge, so that rescue workers could warm their cold hands.

DINNERTIME FOR THE RESCUE WORKERS [90]

One motor boat and 14 row boats made repeated sorties into the district and came back with two or three people each trip. These people were taken to private homes,

---

[90] *The Indianapolis News,* March 29, 1913, Indiana State Library microfilm

given food and drink and put to bed. Most homes outside the flood zone had a number of survivors in them.

Religious Services on a Stranded Train

The Vandalia Railroad's St. Louis to New York train had been due to arrive in Indianapolis Tuesday at 11:45 a.m. There was a slide in the embankment on the west side of the White River, which blocked the train's passage. Over the next day and a half, they were stuck here and decided to get to know each other.

Among the passengers was a preacher from Dayton, Ohio, which had an estimated 1,500 dead. It was decided Wednesday night to have a church meeting in the observation car.

"The pastor prayed", said a Mr. George Schwartzkopf, of Columbus, Indiana. "I wish you could have heard that prayer. I never heard such a pathetic, eloquent and fervent appeal to the Creator in my life."

Water Level in Broad Ripple Falling

This evening, it was reported that the water level in the town of Broad Ripple had fallen 16 inches. You could hear the water rushing back into the White River from a block away. The town was still cut off from all communication except for an occasional phone call. A man on horseback could occasionally get into town.

The 200 flood victims in town were being taken care of by their fellow citizens, being housed in the Broad Ripple Bank, the Red Men's Hall and the schoolhouse.

At 8 pm. the main levee near the locks of the water company was in good shape. It was roped off and guarded, as no one was allowed to set foot on its soft ground. So far, the townspeople were getting enough to eat, but supplies were running low.

Providing Care for the Refugees

Over 200 homeless people, mostly women and children, were housed this evening at the old Zion Church on Ohio Street, near

Illinois. The militia's cots were provided, but there was a call for blankets, clothing and food. The Volunteers of America, supplanted by the Y.M.C.A. assisted in the relief work.

This is only a partial list of the relief organizations and church groups that assisted in this massive operation.

The flood survivors who were taking refuge on the "hill", in West Indianapolis, were by nightfall desperate for food and water, being surrounded by water. Grocery stores had by now been stripped of their stocks.

Coffin Makes Contact

[91] Superintendent Martin Hyland at his desk.

Today, at the Moorefield railroad yards (also known as the Belmont yards), Captain George V. Coffin got a telegraph operator to get a call into his superior, Superintendent Martin Hyland at police headquarters. This was his first communication with Hyland in

---

[91] 1913 IPD Yearbook, Lichtenberger History Room.

three days, police and fire Gamewell lines being knocked out west of the White River.

Coffin estimated there were 6,000 to 8,000 homeless people, all of whom were in need of food. This was the greatest need and he had ordered 3,000 loaves of bread from the Taggart bakery.

Mr. Joseph Taggart refused to do so unless allowed to do so unless the bread was free. The first load of bread left Wednesday evening. Coffin told Hyland he had plenty of coffee.

Coffin had confiscated all food stocks from every grocery and drug store in the sector and parceled them out to hungry people, but by midday Wednesday nearly all grocery stores west of White River were cleaned out.

Captain Coffin felt the list of the dead would exceed 300 when it was complete. Others leaned toward between 20 and 25. Captain Coffin made arrangements with the Big Four Railroad to bring provisions from Crawfordsville, Indiana to the Belmont Railroad yards near the flood zone.

He had four officers from IPD on his side of the river according to *The Indianapolis Star*, March 27, 1913.

One of those officers, Sergeant Harley Reed, said late Wednesday that he and Patrolman Walter H. Cox had rescued nearly 500 persons from flooded areas. He expressed the opinion the death toll would top 100.

"I cannot be sure, after going over nearly every foot of the inundated country in which we confined our efforts yesterday, how everyone could escape.", he said. "I am not in a position to state the number of lives lost but I know that the loss of life must be great. The most pitiful stories of the suffering of the water-bound persons were told as Cox and I proceeded through the district, taking families from the roofs and second stories of every house which we came to. Never, never again will I hear the tales as they were told to me then. We did not discover any bodies." said Sergeant Reed.

Reed said that Father Joseph Weber of the Catholic Church estimated there were 6,000 residents of the west side that were homeless.

Sergeant Harry Franklin spoke to police officials via telephone as well. He described the problems his men had on Monday night when they made their boat trip to bring relief to the refugees at School No. 16.

Franklin also spoke with Mayor Shank, who authorized him on behalf of the Relief Committee, to order grocery supplies from towns and cities west of Indianapolis, which could be contacted.

Saving a Dog's Life - Twice

On the Oliver Avenue Bridge, a policeman saw a spotted hound with one eye in a house, 100 yards away. The officer called to him and the dog got the courage to jump in the water and swim to the levee.

The officer picked him up, put him in a car, heated by a stove and wrapped him in a rug. After an hour, the policeman left the car and saw the dog swimming back to the house. He managed to coax the dog back and sent him to the Indianapolis Abattoir for safe keeping. The house had been vacated Tuesday and the dog was apparently overlooked.

Among the many volunteer boatmen were brothers Jimmy and Herbert Burcham. They watched the flood waters rising from the upper story of Jimmy's home at 813 Arbor Avenue.

They shouted repeatedly to their next-door neighbors Mr. & Mrs. Frank Greiner, who lived in a one-story home, to flee to a taller structure down the street.

When the water got to waist level, the Greiner's, realizing their situation was dire, called for help. They got on top of a table. When the water level got to their necks, their screams for help forced a decision by the Burcham brothers to stop being spectators and become rescuers. Their mother tried to stop them, but they had to act.

They went downstairs and tore off the doors and took them upstairs to their veranda, where they nailed them into a makeshift craft. The Burchams piloted it to the Greiner's home, where the couple were now on the roof.

Jimmy and Herbert got Mrs. Greiner off her own porch roof and onto the craft. As soon as she got on board, it started being taken away by the fast current.

Jimmy pulled her back to safety, while Herbert went after the floating doors. Jimmy then took Mrs. Greiner to a higher building. Herbert and Mr. Greiner then got into the attic, where they were later rescued. The Burchams continued rescuing people on March 27th.

The Last Bridge

Wednesday, March 26, 1913, 9 p.m.

The Oliver Avenue Bridge, in 1910. Postcard.

During the day, a force of men had been working to save the Oliver Avenue Bridge, which was receiving a constant pounding from the flood waters.

Thousands of sand bags and tons of rock were hauled to the west end of the bridge and dumped on the upstream (north) side in attempt to stop it from being undermined.

Police allowed only ambulances and hearses from crossing at this time.

About 9 p.m., a warning cry was given by people walking across the bridge that it was swaying and that it would fail due to the pressure of the water. Captain Hill of the National Guard ordered all of his men across to the east end of the bridge.

About 100 spectators also fled to the east end. Members of the police department also left the west end. The police roped off the east end, refusing to allow anyone to cross, before leaving via the west end of the bridge.

92 Southwest abutment of Oliver Avenue Bridge.

Captain A.J. Perry, commander of Company H of the Indiana National Guard, reported that while his detachment patrolled the east approach to the Oliver Avenue Bridge, he witnessed the concrete abutment north of the bridge crumble. "Then the water rushed into the streets and alleys over there and immediately cries went up from the

---

[92] *The Indianapolis Star*, March 27, 1913. Indiana State Library microfilm

residents. We could see the water in a raging flood, which seemed a mile wide."

This created a serious situation as the Washington Street Bridge, the Vandalia RR and Indianapolis & Vincennes RR bridges had failed and the Morris Street Bridge's western approach had washed out. The Kentucky Avenue Bridge, close to the Oliver Avenue Bridge, had been closed to all traffic as being unsafe.

This left the Big Four Railroad Bridge and the new Vandalia Railroad Bridge. This transit of the former was considered extremely dangerous because the rushing muddy torrent of water was only a few feet from the ties.

It was thought that frightened people trying to walk over the bridge would fall between the ties to certain death. Some people did brave the surviving Vandalia Bridge.

Top: March 27, 1913 photograph of Kingan's Packing Company bridge destroyed. IPD Patrolman Leonard B. Forsythe was said to be the last man to cross this bridge before it was swept away. Postcard.

The bridge used by Kingan & Company, the first north of the Oliver Avenue Bridge, went down into the White River this night. It had been used to move stock across the river.

After the collapse of the approach to the Oliver Avenue Bridge, police would not allow anyone to cross it except refugees and rescue workers. Some of the militia men and police officers on guard on Oliver Avenue had thought that the 10:30 a.m.

levee breech might relieve the pressure on the bridge and save the only remaining means of safe escape from West Indianapolis.

There were suggestions that a cable be anchored over the White River to be used in ferrying the big flatboats to the stricken West Indianapolis area. The possible loss of the Oliver Avenue Bridge made crossing the White River otherwise almost impossible. There was an unknown amount of people stranded, but not in danger of drowning, in this area.

Relief Trip Launched

At 9 p.m., as the Oliver Avenue Bridge started swaying, two boats launched from the bridge. Their purpose was to reach marooned flood victims near Belmont Avenue, north and south of Washington Street.

The group was under the leadership of Bunny Long, iron worker and they carried 500 loaves of bread. The boats were equipped with powerful searchlights provided by Prest-O-Light.

They rowed to the Belt Railroad, being interrupted while crossing six streets and grounding three times on debris. They "shot the rapids" twice where the waters of Eagle Creek were rushing into the bottoms, also known as the "valley".

After an hour, the pilot boat disappeared from view, leaving the second boat, a "cutter", with Bunny Long to make the trip alone with the bread.

They failed to reach the marooned victims past the Belt Railroad, so they made a tour of the entire flood district between the Belt and the White River.

They found a family at 1214 Oliver Avenue who refused to be evacuated, so they left them some bread. Two other homes were found occupied, who also refused relief. The cutter returned to the Oliver Avenue Bridge at 1 a.m. Thursday.

At a late-night meeting of Mayor Shank's general relief committee, organized earlier this day, there was unanimous agreement that they needed to relocate to the bank of the White river, where the suffering was taking place.

Based on incoming reports, it was decided that the flatboats that were hurriedly built that afternoon were not fit for the rescue work. New boats would have to be caulked and painted with white lead and covered with canvass before being used to save lives or hauling supplies. Twenty-five boats were built during the next hours.

The committee decided to do whatever was necessary to provide the means for reaching flood victims with haste, due to the poor weather conditions. Work on getting the existing boats ready for use was started over the next few hours of Thursday morning.

A call for oarsmen to operate them was issued, the men being requested to report to the Mayor's office. The work of the relief committee aided over 3,000 victims of the flood during this evening.

Any owner of an automobile was requested to report to the relief committee at their headquarters in Mayor Shank's office. These vehicles were desperately needed by relief workers. Many people had already been bringing their vehicles in for use during this catastrophe.

Wednesday, March 26, 1913, 10 p.m.

At 10 p.m., rescuers working from the Morris Street Bridge were called in by the police. It was too dangerous for them to continue working without losing their own lives.

Scene at the Claypool Hotel

Earlier in the evening, a man hired an express wagon and went out to the flood district on the west side to help in any way he could. He came back at 10 p.m. and went to the Weber drug store inside the Claypool hotel. He asked a clerk if the store could supply a milk bottle with a nipple attachment.

"Sure," said the clerk.

"Well, and could you warm me some milk and put it in the bottle? You see, there's a little baby out west that hasn't had anything to eat for about two days and I want to kinda help him out," the man said.

The milk was quickly prepared and the man got on his express wagon and headed back west. As he told someone later, "You ought to have heard that baby go after that milk. It certainly makes a fellow feel good. To know you saved a kid suffering. And it was all such a small thing to do, too."

Thursday, March 27, 1913

Sketched from the top of the Merchants Bank Building.

From William T. Riley's journal: *March 27. Cold, snow on ground. Sun shined in the p.m. 4 Engine washed out in stockyard field east of round house. Track cut for 500 feet east of coal warehouse. Did not work today.*

At daylight, IPD Lieutenant Charles Barmfuhrer sent 1,000 loaves of bread and other supplies into the flood zone near the Oliver Avenue Bridge. He instructed the boatmen to only take those suffering from exposure and women and children. Any

---

[93] *The Indianapolis Star*, March 28, 1913. Indiana State Library microfilm

man who had refused to be removed the previous day was to be left until last.

West Indianapolis street car. [94]

The list of potential fatalities as of this morning:

- Woman and baby seen lying in house.
- Unidentified man seen floating in water.

---

[94] From "Twelve Views of the Indianapolis Flood of March 1913" published by C.A. Tutewiler, authors possession.

- Man believed to have been railroad watchman seen to disappear in river.
- Unidentified rescuer reported drowned.
- Unknown infant, seen floating in the water at Warren Avenue by Stanley Faulkner.
- Member of relief corps at Oliver Avenue, pulled from a tree, lifeless.
- Bud Boyd, shoemaker, reported drowned.
- Several persons, imprisoned in an attic, reported dead.

Other reported deaths, which were largely hearsay, included:
- IPD Patrolman George Stone was informed by railroad men that they rescued a man on a raft at Harding Street and the Vandalia railroad tracks. He reported his two companions had drowned.
- A watchman marooned in the tower at the intersection of the Belt Railway and the St. Louis division of the Big Four was seen to walk up the tracks toward Indianapolis. He lost his

balance and was last seen disappearing under the waters.
- A youth, aiding in the rescue in a canoe, believed to have drowned. This is likely the same boy seen drowning in one account in Washington Street when his canoe broke in two.

Nordyke & Marmon Foundry.

[95] Foundry of Nordyke and Marmon Wrecked by Flood, 1913
Indiana Historical Society, P0326

Gauging Station Swept Away.

96

The water gauge station of the United States Weather Bureau, which was located below the West Washington Street Bridge, was washed away by the flood. When Verne H. Church, section director, tried to determine the height of the flood on Wednesday, he had to make estimates from

---

[96] *The Indianapolis Star*, March 27, 1913. Indiana State Library microfilm

the height of the water on familiar buildings.

His estimate was that the crest of the flood was 24.27 feet, over 4 feet higher than the previous record of April 1, 1904. For statistical minded people, since Sunday morning, March 23rd, 6.83 inches of rain had fallen. This equated to 953,491,997,924 cubic inches of water had fallen in Indianapolis, weighing 17,160,030,562 tons. (17.1 billion tons).

Other estimates made the crest 29 feet above flood stage.

A Dangerous Rescue Trip

On the morning of March 27th, five men attempted to rescue residents who were marooned in the neighborhood of the Nordyke & Marmon Automobile Company's plant. The rescue party consisted of citizens "Happy" Wirth, Harry Fehrenbach, Herbert Hyman and E.R. Hisey, along with IPD Mounted Officer Othello Thomas.

They left the Morris Street Bridge in a large motor boat, thinking their craft could stand the treacherous currents flowing into Morris Street. These currents had thwarted previous rescue attempts here. After first patrolling the flooded area on Oliver Avenue, Division Street and Morris Street west of the Belt Railroad, the men carried the boat across the tracks and entered the water east of the railroad.

In midstream the engine quit running. Now they were at the mercy of the current and the boat was dashed against a telegraph pole, then dipped below the surface, half filling with water.

The men desperately held onto the telegraph pole, in an attempt to stay out of the current, until the motor was again started. Travelling on a bit, they again were caught in a strong current from the automobile plant and the engine again quit.

They were carried into a pile of debris and held onto the wood until two canoes could reach them. They were then able to hold onto two telegraph poles. Holding onto the guy wires, they were able to get the boat out of the current again. Attempts to rescue these would-be rescuers failed from men along the shore until finally men in canoes with a rope brought them to shore after 30 minutes of work.

Due to the strong currents pulling the boats out into the street, it was impossible to remove people from these homes. They had to resort to throwing sacks of food onto porches and window sills.

Many of these flood victims said they hadn't had anything to eat or drink for over 24-hours. In many cases where removal was possible, people refused to leave their homes, since water had been receding.

Extended Stay at the Stockyards Hotel

A RESCUE.

97

Later on this date, the men marooned in the Nordyke & Marmon Company were found to be safe when it was possible to approach the plant from the north. Food and water were left with them.

---

97 *The Indianapolis Star*, March 29, 1913. Indiana State Library microfilm

Today was the first time that an organized relief effort was able to enter the West Indianapolis area. The receding White River allowed access from the Oliver Avenue and Morris Street Bridges. They had survived the battering they took during the flood. The Morris Street Bridge was out of plumb, however.

Relief wagons crossed the Morris Street Bridge loaded with provisions for the Indianapolis Abattoir, which was used as a central relief distribution point due to its high ground. A second distribution point was at the Marion Motor Car Company plant, at the west end of the Oliver Street Bridge.

At this time, on Thursday, rescue operations had ceased, no more people were being removed from the flood zone unless at their own request. Instead, manpower was now being concentrated on delivering provisions to the victims.

The Stockyards Hotel was located in the Union Stockyards, on the southwest part of town. The proprietor was George Caldwell. Hotel guests worried about the rising water departed Tuesday morning on the last street car to leave the hotel. Anyone who didn't leave was stuck there for the duration. Early that evening, people living in the "valley" sought refuge at the hotel.

From his vantage point, Caldwell saw the lowlands being flooded and with the help of others, began building boats. The men worked all day Tuesday, building five boats. These boats made rescue trips all over the west part of Indianapolis, until 10 a.m. Thursday.

These people were wet, poorly clad and nearly frozen when they arrived at the hotel. They were given dry clothing and stimulants. Caldwell took care of anyone who couldn't pay for their lodging and meals at his loss.

Eventually, 400 people were staying at the Stockyard Hotel. Caldwell received meat from the John Moore Packing Company and on Thursday, from the Indianapolis Abattoir distribution point.

Modest Hero of the Flood.

WILLARD WYMANN.

[98]

One of the boatmen who launched from the stockyards was Willard Wymann, a young man who made a number of daring trips in a boat that looked flimsy. Onlookers urged him to wait until a stronger boat was found but he left anyway. He was hailed as one of the heroes of the flood.

---

[98] *The Indianapolis Star*, April 3, 1913. Indiana State Library microfilm

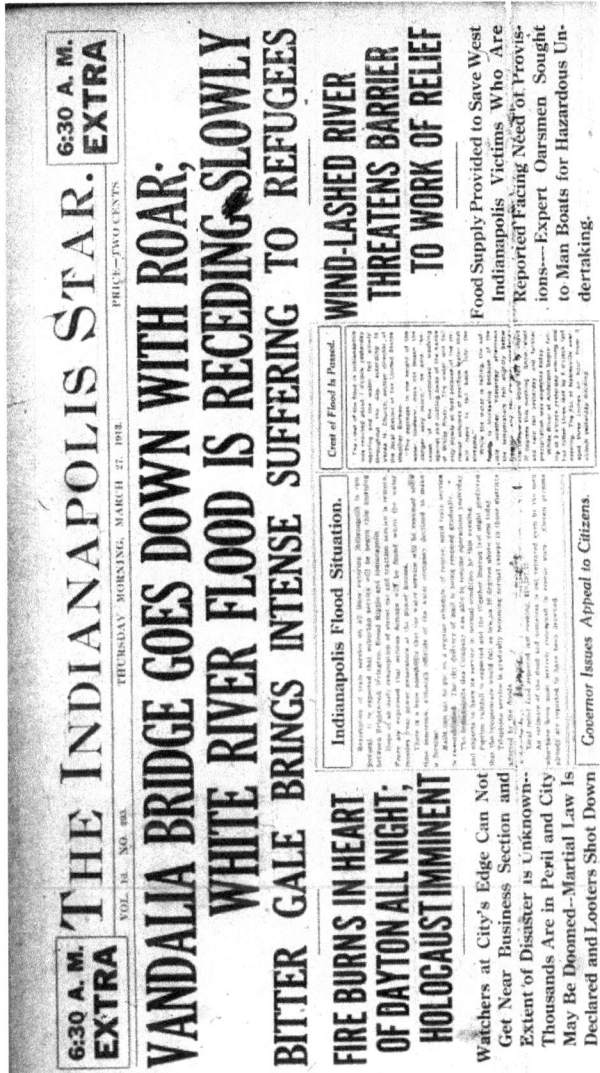

[99] *The Indianapolis Star*, March 27, 1913. Indiana State Library microfilm

Thursday, March 27, 1913, 7 a.m.

The temperature in Indianapolis at 7 a.m. today was 26. It would stay below 29 throughout the early afternoon. The rain had stopped and there was none in the immediate forecast.

Early this morning, a number of passengers from the stranded Vandalia Railroad's St. Louis to New York train walked on the rails to cross the gap in the embankment of the road bed, holding onto the ties. They then walked along the right of way and over the surviving Vandalia Railroad bridge into Indianapolis to get to Union Station that afternoon, about 48 hours late.

Sergeant Harley Reed, sick from exposure, was sent home in a boat, on this day. Police sent out a patrol wagon filled with boots to the flood district early today. Superintendent Hyland sent 50 pair to the men whose boots were leaking badly.

After Captain Kruger of IPD was notified this date that two carloads of cattle on a siding at Beecher Street and the Belt

Railroad were dying, he sent word to Humane Officer Oscar Merrill. Merrill found three railroad carloads of cattle and hogs there. Nine hogs had died.

He arranged for a switch engine to transport them to the Abattoir Company, so they could be fed and watered. This car had left Fortville on Tuesday. Captain Kruger, who reported for duty at 3 p.m. Tuesday, had been on duty since then, getting four hours of sleep.

Signs of Civilization

The situation in Indianapolis on Thursday morning was that the resumption of interurban service would begin in the morning between Indianapolis and the suburb neighborhoods of Brightwood, Irvington and Broad Ripple.

However, the street car and traction service was still down and there were fears that when the water receded from the power generators, that serious damage would be found. People had been walking home from work or catching a ride on any wagon or car that they could find, since noon on Tuesday.

There was a slim hope that water service would start sometime Friday. On Thursday morning, officials of the Indianapolis Water Company were informed that the White River had fallen four feet since late yesterday and Fall Creek had fallen 4.5 feet. If the White River fell another two feet, they could start the furnaces of its Riverside plant.

Town pump, Massachusetts Avenue and Delaware Street.

Since Tuesday, citizens of Indianapolis had been relying on water from various wells in Indianapolis, including the fountains at the Monument Circle. Lines had been long. A local distiller had provided free distilled water upon request.

The only street pump in the business district of Indianapolis was located at

---

[100] *The Indianapolis Star*, March 27, 1913. Indiana State Library microfilm

Massachusetts Avenue and Delaware Street. It was in use constantly Wednesday.

The city street cleaning department was now working night and day to haul drinking water to shelters and hospitals. They had 12 large tank wagons, working shifts with new men and mules.

They were getting the water from the Wheeler & Schebler plant on Shelby Street, which was pumping it from a 400 foot deep well. The American Brewing Company also was offering drinking water to anyone who needed it, at their warehouse on West Ohio Street.

The Indianapolis Gas Company resumed operations on Wednesday and expected their service to get back to normal by this evening. The United States mail service had been severely curtailed until recently, due to the lack of train operations in town.

The first mail to arrive in Indianapolis since the flood became dangerous, arrived by automobile from Franklin, Indiana on March 26th. By March 27th, 60 truckloads of mail were piled up at the Union Station in Indianapolis, waiting to be shipped out.

Telephone service was reportedly normal except in the flood zones. The lines had been jammed in the early part of the flood. This morning, the citizens of Indianapolis were facing a shortage of fresh meats, eggs and butter, according to people familiar with the food situation.

This was due to the lack of train service. There was no shortage of potatoes in Indianapolis, according to Mr. W.H. Roberts, of the W.H. Roberts & Co. commission house.

He said the only "potato famine" was of the round white potato that restaurants were out of. The supply of these was gone but there were plenty of seed potatoes on hand, which were red-skinned, but "cook white and are good to eat." There were also plenty of beans in the city.

The Weather Bureau predicted more rain and temperatures in Indianapolis would fall to 20 degrees above zero Thursday.

The General Emergency Committee had received $12,000 in donations as of this morning.

Coffin's Headquarters

Photograph of the makeshift headquarters of the Indianapolis Police Department and the National Guard. It was once used by members of the Socialist Party and was on Belmont Avenue near the tracks of the C.H. & D. Railroad. General Garrard, in charge of the militia, is on right. Captain George V. Coffin is 3rd from left.

By Thursday, the floodwaters were clearly receding. But they were uncovering the muddy wreckage of entire neighborhoods. Many weeks of cleanup and reconstruction lay ahead.

When local newspaper reporters found Coffin on Thursday, he was in his makeshift headquarters in a shack on Belmont Avenue at the Cincinnati, Hamilton and Dayton railroad tracks. Coffin was storing meat, flour and other provisions in churches and other buildings. He was feeding the hungry and giving clothes to the naked.

He got a message through to Superintendent Hyland by sending a messenger to Ben Davis (far west side of town), which sent a telegram to St. Louis, relayed to Chicago, then to Indianapolis police headquarters.

Coffin, normally attired in a pressed captain's uniform was wearing an old blue army shirt and "plug" hat. A cigar was in one corner of his mouth. He was busy - "awful busy", he said. When someone said he was a "hero", he frowned or blushed.

Coffin was interviewed by local papers and said "Since the flood began I have seen people drowned on account of the capsizing of boats, and I have seen many bodies floating down stream in the swift currents. I have tried to keep count of the number of bodies I have seen in the water and I estimate that I have seen at least fifty of them.

In my opinion, the number of dead on account of the floods west of the river will far exceed fifty. "I know they were drowned. They were the men we left on roofs when we took women and children out. When we got back for them they were gone. There was only one place for them to have gone."

Asked what day he first came out into the flood, he replied, "Let's see – What day's today? I've lost count."

Coffin moved his headquarters on March 28th to 244 North Elder Avenue (next page), which was closer to the flooded areas.

POLICE AND NEWSPAPER HEADQUARTERS IN HAUGHVILLE DISTRICT

[101] Coffin's headquarters at 244 North Elder Avenue

Captain Coffin swore in 37 citizens as special police officers to patrol the flood zone on this date.

As described by *The Indianapolis Star* on April 14th:

"And such a police department! Never again may there be one similar: Cripples, one-eyed men, derelicts and bums, school teachers

---

[101] *The Indianapolis News*, April 5, 1913, microfilm at Indiana State Library.

and clerks, proofreaders and dairymen were represented in that motley array. And their service was excellent. Their pride took them by the hand and led them straightforwardly along the path of duty."

Charles Gollnisch

They were placed under the command of a patrolman, Bicycleman Charles Gollnisch. They were to be issued badges and clubs on March 28th. They worked effectively in the boats they were assigned to.

Left to right: Bicycleman Charles Gollnisch, Captain George V. Coffin and Bicycleman Thomas O'Brien.

Gollnisch's official title during the crisis was "Chief". During it, he earned the title by his display of executive ability.

Dr. E.A. Willis, secretary to the mayor's advisory committee, issued a call this night for all who had passed the civil service examination for positions with the police department, to report to City Hall immediately to be sworn in as special police.

A Trip to the Ball Park

Five professional ball players, Charles O'Leary and Ed Galloway of the Indianapolis Indians (American Association minor league team) and Steve Evans, Lee Magee and Polly Perritt, of the St. Louis Cardinals, decided to take a trip to Washington Park, home of the Indians this day.

It was considered a dangerous trip even as flood waters were receding. They first tried to walk across the Vandalia railroad bridge but were turned back by officials for lack of credentials. They then boarded a switch engine making its first trip to the flood district and rode across the same bridge.

They had to view the park from the railroad on the south but got a good view of the damage, mainly to the bleachers and the fences, all of the former being down and the bleachers destroyed except for the left side. Washington Park was located at 1235 West Washington Street. This is now the location of the Indianapolis Zoo. That morning, two feet of water remained on the grounds.

Later in the afternoon, Manager Mike Kelley via the Vandalia Bridge, accompanied by a team of workmen who went about making repairs. He was optimistic that the team could start practicing Saturday, thinking the diamond would dry out in a few hours. He was mistaken as by Saturday, it was decided that they would travel to St. Louis to practice and wouldn't return to Indianapolis until April 24th.

Thursday, March 27, 1913, 8 a.m.

At 8 a.m., soldiers and others standing on the Morris Street Bridge watched as the body of a woman, face down, floated under it.

JAMES A COLLINS
Judge of the City Court

In police court, Judge Collins had a parade of flood victims come before him. Fred Vanlandingham and John Barton had rescued an old woman from her West Indianapolis home. Then they went downtown, had some drinks and then Barton tried to cash a check.

Due to his condition, it wasn't cashed and Barton was arrested by Bicyclemen Long

---

[102] 1913 IPD Yearbook, Lichtenberger History Room.

and Sheridan at the bank. Vanlandingham tried to prevent Barton's arrest, so he was charged also.

Charles Cook, a flood refugee from west Morris Street, was arrested by Patrolman Jesse McMurtry for intoxication. Judge Collins warned him not to drink anymore. Saying "There is enough distress in the city without making it any harder for these unfortunate men who got themselves in trouble," Collins released Vanlandingham and Burton as well.

[103] Break in Levee on White River, Indianapolis, Flood March 27, 1913
Indiana Historical Society, P0391

Thursday, March 27, 1913, 10 a.m.

FRANK ROW,
Sergeant of Police.

IPD Sergeant Frank E. Row was in charge of the work done at the Oliver Street Bridge after 10 a.m. He directed the boats leaving with provisions and also served as an early version of a Public Information Officer, answering numerous questions.

---

[104] 1913 IPD Yearbook, Lichtenberger History Room.

One man in a boat was trying to reach the persons at Wulf's Hall when his craft got stuck in a yard with a high fence. The receding waters brought him down so he was now stuck inside and he rowed around for two hours trying to find the gate, to no avail. Arrangements were made to get him out in another boat.

Rockets used to Restore Telephone Cables

This photograph apparently shows the operation of shooting a rocket across the White River on March 27, 1913. Looking east toward Indianapolis from the west side of the White River.

---

[105] Washington Street Bridge from the West Side After Flood had Receded, March 1913. Indiana Historical Society, P0326

When the Washington Street Bridge failed Wednesday morning, it took all of the telephone company's cables with it as well as those supplying power. This cut off telephone communication west of the river with the rest of Indianapolis.

To reconnect the Belmont exchange with the rest of the city, a rocket was fired across White River from the east approach at noon Thursday. It carried a small cord on it, the other end remaining on the east side.

Linemen from the Central Union Telephone Company had previously made their way in a roundabout manner, to the west side of the river and grabbed the line when it landed. The men on the east side then attached a heavier cord to the string and to this was attached a heavier wire, known as a messenger. These were pulled across the White River.

They also connected the wires of the Indianapolis Light & Heat Company to supply current for the Belmont exchange to the "messenger".

Paving blocks washed out on North Meridian Street.

---

[106] Paving Blocks Washed Out During Flood, N. Meridian Street, Indianapolis, 1913. Indiana Historical Society, P0326

As the waters of Fall Creek dropped by a foot, severe damage was revealed in the fashionable neighborhood north of that stream. The homes were bounded by Illinois Street on the west, College Avenue on the east and on the north by 31st Street. Only a few people were found, working on their homes.

Hardwood floors were ruined and furnaces knocked out. Residents were staying with relatives or in downtown hotels. The pavement blocks on Illinois and Meridian Streets, up to 28th Street, was destroyed.

Humane Officer Oscar Merrill and Councilman Stilz caught two suspected looters in a West Indianapolis home Thursday. Fred Cline, 20 and George Johnson, 18, were caught with a quantity of tobacco. Cline also had a ring full of skeleton keys on him. Both were locked up in the city jail at police headquarters.

When they made their appearance before Judge Collins, they said they had been working for two days in canoes taking people from their homes and while rowing past a grocery they saw some tobacco packages floating inside. They used their oars to get it. Collins released them.

Thursday, March 27, 1913, 4 p.m.

Pat Rooney Dances for Flood Sufferers

Vaudevillian Pat Rooney, in town for a benefit performance at the English Opera House Friday, spent an hour starting at 4 p.m. selling copies of *The Indianapolis News* in the city streets. Followed by a large wagon with a band, carrying streamers saying the money collected would go to flood victims, Rooney was dressed as a newsboy. He danced a jig for the crowd and then sold papers for whatever they would bring, from nickels to $5 each. He sold 600 copies in an hour for $80.

The Fletcher Savings & Trust Company, one of the leading banks in Indianapolis, announced today that depositors could withdraw money without losing interest.

Workers are unloading food in the Cincinnati, Hamilton & Dayton Railroad Yards on Belmont Street. Bread from the Taggart Bakeries, supplied to the refugees, is on the wagon.

---

[107] Unloading Supplies for Flood Sufferers C.H. & D Yards Belmont Street, Indiana Historical Society, P0391

A special train from Danville, Indiana, to the west of Indianapolis, carried supplies into the railroad yards off of Belmont Street this date. Father Weber and the military authorities took charge of this shipment.

Another carload of hams, potatoes, flour and other provisions from Crawfordsville, arrived on Holmes Avenue via the T.H.L. & E. interurban line in the afternoon and was distributed. These items went to Captain Coffin's "colony", the refugees who had previously been at School No. 16.

Swift & Company, meat packers from Chicago, sent a car load of meat for Indianapolis flood victims. This meat was unloaded this evening and made available Friday for distribution.

Captain Coffin found a working telephone at the home of I.E. Beere, 1130 Blaine Avenue Thursday, after wading for blocks. The telephone was turned over to police and newspaper reporters.

Police Rescue Detail. Captain George V. Coffin is believed to be 2nd from left. [108]

---

[108] Postcard belonging to author.

School House Number 16, March 27, 1913.

[109] *The Indianapolis Star*, March 28, 1913. Indiana State Library microfilm.

One of the last people to be rescued from West Indianapolis this date was John Hughey, an elderly man who was found by Jimmy and Herbert Burcham while they were giving Charles Murphy, IFD fireman and Patrick Hilroy, a boat ride from "the hill" to the Oliver Avenue Bridge.

They discovered him near death at 1122 River Avenue. Against Hughey's wishes, Murphy and Hilroy lowered him from the second floor to a veranda roof and into the rowboat.

Hughey, who passed out during the rescue, was wrapped in blankets and rowed to the landing at Morris Street and Blaine Avenue, where he was revived. Hughey had been one of the people who refused to be rescued, thinking he could ride the flood out. The cold weather and lack of food took their toll on him.

Scammers Paradise

Mayor Shank walked into Tomlinson Hall this afternoon and a busy woman among the charity workers approached him.

"Mr. Mayor, the organization in this hall is something awful. Nobody knows how to take charge and things are not run right at all."

Shank replied, "Well, maybe you're right. I'll just appoint you the manager of the whole shebang to suit yourself."

He walked a few feet away and another woman volunteer came to him. The same conversation ensued. He appointed her the chief of the relief workers. By the time he left, he had made at least a dozen women happy.

Shank then walked down Alabama Street to police headquarters. After being there a few minutes, a call came in that there were "too many bosses" in Tomlinson hall and that a dozen women had been ejected from the hall. The mayor said, "just a little joke."

Det. Sgt. Chauncey A. Manning

There were opportunists during this crisis. This date, a man named Arrol Beeler, 32, from out of town, volunteered as a helper at Tomlinson Hall. He was stopped by Detectives Manning and Cronin trying to leave with two new suits of clothes, two overcoats, all of which he was wearing

---

[110] 1913 IPD Yearbook, Lichtenberger History Room.

except two pairs of shoes in a package. Beeler, a traveling "evangelistic minister" had a Bible and $23 in cash on his person. He admitted to not being carried out of the flood zone in a boat but being from McClainsville. He was charged with grand larceny.

J. CRONIN,
Detective Sergeant.

---

[111] 1913 IPD Yearbook, Lichtenberger History Room.

Manning and Cronin also apprehended Louis B. Wilson, age 22. He was stopped leaving Tomlinson Hall by the rear with a suit case full of clothing. He said the suit case was his. It had the name of "Mitchell" on it, the name of a traveling man held up in Indianapolis by the flood. Wilson was charged with petit larceny.

Another con artist nabbed by Manning and Cronin Thursday was Alva Christian, 22. He went to Tomlinson Hall, telling a sorrowful tale of loss and was given food and shelter.

He left Friday morning with two shirts, two silk handkerchiefs and a gold pin belonging to Walter Wood, custodian of the mission. He was locked up and charged with petit larceny. He was from out of town.

Looting Begins in West Indianapolis

[112] Left to right: Major W.H. Kershner, inspector-general, Captain P.A. Davis, Captain H.A. Lucky, Sergeant L.B. Jarrett. The guardsmen were near headquarters at Belmont Avenue and the C.H.&D. Railway, following a visit to the stations of the militiamen for the purposes of a medical inspection.

---

[112] *The Indianapolis News*, March 29, 1913. Indiana State Library microfilm

This afternoon, four men were arrested on the Morris Street Bridge by militiamen. They were suspected of looting. One, Archibald Cantwell had a razor on him and was arrested for carrying a concealed weapon. The other three were released.

When officers of IPD and the militia took a boat tour through the flooded district Thursday, they saw much evidence of looting in the Union Stock Yards.

Numerous windows above the water line were broken and evidence of canoes being pulled through them so the thieves could work unseen, were found.

By today, reports were filtering in to the Relief Committee of price gouging, or "extortion" as it was called in *The Indianapolis Star*. Bread was selling for 20 cents a loaf and milk for 20 cents a quart in West Indianapolis.

The flip side of this story was an advertisement in the *Star* on March 28th by the E.A. Kirk Bakery, selling bread at 4 cents a loaf for the next two weeks.

A story of a young woman stranded at Union Station with 36 cents in her purse paying 5 cents on one day and 10 cents the next day, for a cup of coffee, was related. Restaurants were also accused of this. The mayor said he could do nothing until the governor declared martial law. In coming days, severe steps to curb this would be considered, enforced by the Indianapolis Police Department.

Thursday, March 27, 1913, 5 p.m.

The water level of the White River had fallen from between four and five feet from the high-water mark at 7 a.m. today. It fell slower at the Marion Motor Car Company, a total of about 18 inches today. At the Indianapolis Water Company's Riverside pumping station, measurements taken at 5 p.m. showed the water level had receded five feet from its maximum height. The company promised the residents of Indianapolis water on Friday.

Confusion at the Oliver Avenue Bridge

As the flood water began to recede, control over who got into the West Indianapolis area became very confused. Things were running pretty smoothly when controlled by the National Guard and IPD Lieutenant Charles Barmfuhrer at the Oliver Avenue Bridge, gateway to the flood zone.

A group of citizens was formed to assist the workers and they began issuing passes to anyone wishing to return to their homes.

The police were also empowered to pass through anyone they wished. So did Mayor Shank and Superintendent Hyland. A flood of returning refugees began, congesting the Oliver Avenue Bridge.

Lieutenant J.W. Hill of the 2nd Infantry made an appeal to the Mayor, explaining the problem. He was then given sole authority to issue passes, all the others being rescinded. Within an hour in the late afternoon, the bridge was cleared and work, which had been interrupted, began again.

Lt. Hill and Lt. Barmfuhrer worked well together.

Governor Ralston had a proclamation written declaring all of West Indianapolis under martial law, in order to prevent looting of the hundreds of deserted homes in this flood zone. He then decided to forestall issuing it unless necessary. Two companies of the Indiana National Guard were sent to Indianapolis at once. He made this decision after conferring with Superintendent of Police Martin Hyland.

Many of the residents of West Indianapolis who were denied passes after this called Governor Ralston to complain and asked that he issue passes. Since there was no martial law, the Ralston deferred to Superintendent Hyland. Hyland would later remove all restrictions.

Members of the Indiana National Guard were deployed late in the afternoon Thursday in West Indianapolis. For its part, the police department had set up a strict border around the flood district and they allowed no one to enter or leave who couldn't identify themselves and why they were there. All saloons west of the river were ordered closed by IPD.

The Indiana Album: Barbara Stevens Collection

[113] West Maryland Street on west side of the White River, March 27, 1913. This was close to White River and just south of Washington Street. Bottom photograph is of the same view, farther back.

The Indiana Album: Barbara Stevens Collection

---

[113] The Indiana Album: Barbara Stevens Collection.
[114] Ibid.

In the aftermath of the flood into West Indianapolis, a resident, Dr. John S. Hollingsworth, 1258 Oliver Avenue, gave an interview to *The Indianapolis News*.

"I have been repeatedly to the board of works, to the city engineer and to the other city officials and told them we would have a Johnstown flood situation in Indianapolis if the narrowing of the river on the east bank was not stopped.

"The land grabbers have been busy filling up the low land there and gradually extending it into the river bed, and the manufacturing establishments have been dumping cinders and other stuff into the river, cutting down on its width and making more land to build on. All anyone has to do is to go down to the river and he will see what has been done."

Setting up Soup Kitchens

On Thursday, Captain Coffin ordered that five cars of provisions sitting on railroad sidings at the Cincinnati, Hamilton and Dayton railroad yard on Belmont Avenue be broken into. Coffin confiscated the meat from one box car and it was cooked that night in the ovens of Central Hospital. He believed this was a necessary action as many people were suffering from hunger and there was no way to get it from across the river. The food was divided equally between the churches filled with refugees.

Thursday, March 27, 1913, 6 p.m.

Captain Coffin issued orders from his headquarters on Belmont Avenue to issue portions of the rations. The size of the family determined the portions. Each mouth was allotted two potatoes, a loaf of bread to each three persons, etc. Jake Flick, a baker at 2021 West Washington Street and his staff had been baking bread at all hours, providing thousands of loaves for the victims. He now provided a 30-

gallon caldron which was used to serve soup at a church.

Bread lines were begun in West Indianapolis beyond the flood zone this date. There was still a wide body of water separating them from civilization to the east, so they were dependent on food and water from the west, such as from Crawfordsville and other towns. One of the first bread lines set up by the police and militia was at Morris and Reiner Streets.

By 6 p.m. fifty people were standing in line waiting for the food to be distributed. Another food supply station was at the Odd Fellow's Building a few blocks north of Morris and Reiner. Three more were placed in other parts of West Indianapolis. All were crowded.

[115] Wulf's Hall relief station.

One of the relief stations was Wulf's Hall, above Max Kiefer's saloon, located at 1202 Nordyke. Thursday, there were four women, six men and three children staying here. A relief boat was sent from the Oliver Avenue Bridge to check on them and bring provisions if necessary, this morning.

At 6 p.m., two companies of National Guardsmen arrived and began patrolling West Indianapolis, north of Washington Street this evening. Battery A of the guard took charge south of Washington Street.

---

[115] Wulf's Hall Relief Station, Indianapolis, Ind., Flood March 1913. Indiana Historical Society, P0391

Captain Coffin took charge north of Washington Street.

Thursday, March 27, 1913, 7 p.m.

The Indiana Album: Barbara Stevens Collection

[116] Oliver Avenue after the water level receded March 27th.

The Indianapolis News published this list of those thought to be dead this evening:

• George Smith, volunteer boatman, capsized in rescue work, and after being pulled from the river, clinging to tree branches near Oliver and Holly Avenues, was taken to the hospital. He had done

---

[116] The Indiana Album: Barbara Stevens Collection.

great work saving others and was reported to have later died from exposure.

- William Geyer, attempted to swim from home, was thought to have drowned. Geyer was a teamster and kept his team of horses in a barn at his home. As was learned later, Geyer, who lived at 1310 North Nordyke Avenue, tried to swim, taking two horses out of the flood. He and the horses were caught in the current and disappeared. His body hadn't been recovered as of Thursday evening.

Their report on this subject showed that an extensive survey of the West Indianapolis area made in a canoe, showed no bodies, now that you could see through first story windows. The men who had been working for days in this area in boats estimated there would be a "dozen or so" drowning victims.

The Militia Deployed

Maintaining Order in Flood District.

GUARDSMAN ON DUTY ON MORRIS STREET.

[117]

---

[117] *The Indianapolis Star,* March 28, 1913. Indiana State Library microfilm

Beginning at nightfall tonight, National guardsmen and police were instructed to permit no persons within the flooded territory unless they presented credentials and had business there or were performing rescue work.

This was done to prevent looting. All boats of rescuers were ordered off the water and it was ordered that anyone found in the flood zone without authority should be arrested.

Patrolman Samuel B. Young

There had been numerous reports of looting in the Oliver Avenue area and at 7 p.m.

---

[118] Lichtenberger History Room.

Thursday, Patrolman Sam Young caught up with two suspected looters in a canoe. They were identified as Walter Kimball and Carl Knotts.

Police had given them authority to take a man named Stratton to his home. Shortly after leaving the dock, Kimball and Knotts started to rock the boat, forcing Stratton to jump out. He was later picked up by another boat and reported this to police.

The family of Fred Moore had been driven to the attic of their home on River Avenue, near White River. On the night of March 27th, Patrolmen Guy Harper and Thomas McCoy rescued them. They hadn't had food or water for two days. The officers then broke into a nearby home and found a dead horse in the kitchen.

Funeral Directors Support Sufferers

Three representatives of the city's 33 funeral directors, H.D. Tutewiler, James Bailey and Frank M. McNeely, contacted the general relief committee and told them that the undertakers of Indianapolis would give victims taken from flood zones a proper burial without charge. The committee gave a vote of thanks to the undertakers.

The water levels in "Dogtown", on the southwest side of Indianapolis, went down rapidly this evening and many of the families moved back into their flooded homes. Several still were under two feet of water, but were occupied.

Rescuing station at the Maines Homestead.

---

[119] *The Indianapolis Star, March 28, 1913.* Indiana State Library microfilm

Lt. Charles Barmfuhrer, who was on the Oliver Avenue Bridge this night, put out three patrol boats, each manned by two men in plain clothes, who were instructed to watch for looters.

Four men were brought to police headquarters on a charge of looting Thursday afternoon and evening on the 27th.

Thursday, March 27, 1913, 11 p.m.

Relief work went on late into the night. The relief committee sent a train bearing supplies to the west side by the Belt Railroad. These supplies were then hand carried a ½ mile to the estimated 15,000 people now staying on "the hill" in West Indianapolis.

They were given bread, coffee, sugar, canned goods and blankets. Captain Thomas F. Ryan of the local army recruiting station said that the area was seriously in need of protection because of many "ruffians" stealing everything in sight.

There were robberies occurring. He said the military were taking steps to prevent this. By tomorrow morning it would be reported that the men under Captain Coffin and 42 guardsmen had put an end to this.

Lieutenant Barmfuhrer and Sergeant John M. Hett of IPD made an inspection trip over the flooded district from the Oliver Avenue bridge. They took 100 loaves of bread to the refugees under the care of Father Joseph Weber at his church, Church of the Assumption, 1117 Blaine Avenue.

JOHN HETT,
Sergeant of Police.

[120]

They found no bodies on their trip and saw no looters. John M. Hett was credited with numerous rescues during this disaster, taking a number of people from their rooftops and working 18-20 hours a day.

A Mysterious Light

A number of men on watch on the east side of the White River on Michigan Street

---

[120] 1913 IPD Yearbook, Lichtenberger History Room.

Thursday night were puzzled by a mysterious light that seemed to be west of the West Michigan Street Bridge. It was stationary and dim, as if distant. They decided it must be an oil lamp or lantern, probably in a street car west of the bridge.

There had been a street car at the east end of Michigan Street which had been submerged up to the lower edge of the windows, now was 100 feet away from the water's edge.

Carrying Nurse to Refugees.

NURSES WERE CARRIED ACROSS THE BELT AT MORRIS STREET TO ATTEND PERSONS SUFFERING FROM EXPOSURE DURING THE FLOOD.

[121]

---

[121] *The Indianapolis Star*, March 29, 1913. Indiana State Library microfilm

Nurses were transported at 11 p.m. to the Oliver Avenue Bridge to be transported to care for the sick at the Red Men's Hall. Word was received tonight that Captain Chittock of the Indiana National Guard was on his way to Indianapolis from Frankfort, Indiana. He was bringing with him eight army ambulances drawn by four horses, 54 men and four surgeons.

The relief committee adopted a strict rule of "relief, not charity." Anything that they issued to flood victims was to be considered relief, kept separate from work done by the city's charitable organizations, of which there were many.

Captain Coffin ordered all saloons in the flood district to remain closed Thursday. Anyone disobeying orders would be arrested. A meat station for flood sufferers was set up on Harding Street, near Morris Street. Coffin had seized a wagon load of beef belonging to a Chicago firm and placed it in the room. Flood victims were given the option to pay for the meat if they wanted to, but otherwise, it was free.

Friday, March 28, 1913

From William T. Riley's journal: *March 28. Warm for March. Sunshine all day. No work. 3 foot of water on Morris Street and Harding Street. Two days we had no mail.*

7 a.m.

The temperature in Indianapolis at 7 a.m. was 25 degrees. The rescue work in the morning was impeded by ice about ½ inch thick. Canoes couldn't be used, only rowboats. Near the Belt Railroad and Belmont Avenue, the rescuers were wading through the falling water, while making a house to house search for bodies.

All reports so far had not found any bodies in the flood zones and the opinion of all who were knowledgeable of the situation was that the death toll was between 20 and 25.

The Indianapolis Star praised Captain George V. Coffin Friday morning and the work of his assistants. It was now believed about 1,000 flood victims had been taken from residences under water.

The Star credited Coffin with setting up a police force, a health board, a commissary and a hospital west of the White River. In their words, *"the wheels of temporary government ran smoothly under the direction of this one man. With only three or four officers to assist him, but with hundreds of willing, faithful and heroic citizens, questions which have been known to perplex cities in the time of calamity were solved."*

Captain Coffin listed the men who were directly responsible for the rescue work so far:

- Cass Connaway, attorney
- J.E. Settles, railroad brakeman
- Edward M. Colla
- William R. Harryman, deputy clerk of Superior Court
- Jack Cullup, yardmaster at Big Four Railroad
- James Lamkins, deputy city clerk
- Harry M. Franklin, drillmaster of the police department.

"Cass Connaway worked in that freezing water until he was blue, and hardly able to walk," said Coffin. "I had to make him quit, and later, I had to prevent him from making a trip down the river that would have proved disastrous. There is nothing to it, at all, but that the heroism displayed over here has been greater than ever recorded in fiction."

Continuing, Coffin said about Mr. Colla, "This man Colla displayed more nerve than I had ever believed one could hold. He did things that seemed impossible and I have seen him make trips which I thoroughly believed would result in his death. Not only did he work this way for hours but he kept it up for two days and two nights. That man must be made of iron.

William R. Harryman & Sgt. Harry Franklin.

"Mr. Harryman and Mr. Lamkins also displayed great courage. Mr. Lamkins was working under a terrific strain all the time because his family was in the flooded district and he had not heard of their condition. Mr. Cullop, the train master out here, is a man too big for the load he was holding. He has displayed wonderful courage and foresight in the manner he has handled the situation.

---

[122] *The Indianapolis News*, April 2, 1913, p.4. Indiana State Library microfilm.

Coffin described a near death experience for he and Lamkins. "We had struck a powerful current and I was at the oars. Finally, I gave out completely. I could not row another stroke. I turned the oars over to Lamkins and he started off. Suddenly the boat was swerved into a terrific current, which must have been traveling at least 50 miles an hour. Lamkins lost control of the boat and its side struck a telephone pole with great force. There was a crash and we found ourselves in the water. The boat floated away in two parts.

"Lamkins 'skinned' the pole and luckily, I grabbed the guy wire. I was getting to the point where holding was mighty hard work when I ventured to swim a short distance to the corner of a house. I made it all right and soon after I grabbed an oar that was floating past. Lamkins grabbed the other end. Shortly after this we were lucky enough to be rescued by another boat that happened our way."

Situation Improving Across Indianapolis

At 7:30 a.m. Friday, the situation in Indianapolis was improving. The White River and Fall Creek were continuing to fall at a rapid pace. It had fallen an estimated 10 feet from its high point. Street car service had been resumed on the College Avenue, east 10th Street, Brookside Avenue, Irvington and Shelby Street lines.

Power obtained from the plant of the Crawfordsville line was used to get the West Michigan Street and the Illinois Street lines running again.

Railroad officials hoped to have trains running in several directions today, to relieve the mail delivery situation and carry marooned passengers. Water was available for fire protection and it was expected that the water would be turned on for consumer use sometime today. However, it still needed to be boiled for human consumption.

The weather forecast was fair and as of last evening, $32,523.98 had been collected by the relief fund. President Woodrow Wilson sent a telegram to Governor Ralston Thursday:

"I have directed the secretary of war to proceed at once to the flood districts with the necessary staff in order to extend every possible assistance to the sufferers more promptly than would be possible if they had to overcome the present imperfect means of communication. I deeply sympathize with the people of your state in the terrible disaster that has overcome them."

Woodrow Wilson

Much Confusion in Reported Deaths

There were two reported flood deaths. One was Philip Reichart, 80, a German immigrant who had been removed from 333 Beauty Avenue on Tuesday evening to City Hospital. He died of tuberculosis Thursday evening. His death was induced by exposure. He boarded on Beauty Avenue and his only relatives were in Germany.

Also dying Thursday night was a 7-month old son of Mr. & Mrs. Alec Oltean, 1007 West Morris Street. Mother and son had been confined for hours in their tiny attic, where the water finally reached them. They were nearly drowned when rescued.

The child died of pneumonia due to exposure. Relief worker Edward M. Colla, 30, a railroad conductor, had been working side by side with police since the flood. He stated there were not less than 25 dead over Tuesday and Wednesday.

Another reported drowning was that of an unidentified man who was swimming from building to building near Bank Avenue and Ohio Street. He was heading to higher ground until an out building to which he was clinging sank under his weight. He did not reappear.

Two men reported drowned were found alive. Charles Rogers' boat had split in two on March 25th at 9 a.m. around Washington and Bloomington Streets, west of the river.

On Friday morning, the Indianapolis Star announced that his boat was going to the rescue of three men clinging to a telephone pole guy wire that day and one of the crew sank. He was a sailor.

Rogers swam to the guy wire and was later rescued and taken to the Marion Motor Company's plant, where he was given dry clothing. It was the sailor who was now believed dead.

Also found alive was William Geyer, of Nordyke Avenue, reported drowned while trying to save two horses. He was found at the home of J.D. Shelley, 1961 Bellefontaine, in serious condition.

After abandoning his horses near Morris Street, Geyer managed to find a place of safety where he was found by a rescuing party and also taken to the Marion Motor Car Company. He was then sent to the Shelley home after thawing out. The bodies of his horses were found in Morris Street.

Saloon keeper James W. Cline, last seen Tuesday evening working underneath his automobile as flood waters rushed toward him from the Morris Street levee, turned out to be alive and well. He said he managed to get into his saloon when the water came near. He was found later by boatmen.

By Friday, while relief efforts were concentrated in West Indianapolis, police and guardsmen felt that when known, the greater number of fatalities would be found north of Washington Street. The water was deeper here in an area known as "Stringtown", north to Riverside Park.

The reason few fatalities were found in West Indianapolis was that only a few homes were completely submerged, allowing most people the opportunity to climb to the second floor or the roof.

Early comparison of the rescues in West Indianapolis and Stringtown this date was that there were more boats and men working in West Indianapolis. When the Washington Street Bridge went down, it cut off any attempts to reach the area due west and north of the bridge. It was up to Coffin, Franklin and the few men they had to try and save the people.

Examination of the structures after the water went down indicated that the few homes that collapsed were near White River and the broken levees in West Indianapolis. In Stringtown, floating homes and other buildings that came down the White River smashed into homes and did greater damage.

Experienced river men said many of the dead would never be found, having floated downstream in buildings that broke apart, their fate never to be learned.

The first house to be searched by Captain Tyndall of the National Guard and Sergeant Franklin today was 1107 Harding Street, where on Tuesday, Father Joseph F. Weber had believed a family was trapped and drowned.

The second house they wanted to check was 809 Division Street. An entire family is believed to have perished here of drowning or exposure. Tyndall and Franklin attempted entry last night but couldn't get in. The Father also thought two other homes in that block may contain bodies of people who couldn't get out in time.

Harding Street in Indianapolis, Indiana as the water started to recede Thursday, March 27, 1913. *Courtesy Engineering News Volume 69.*

When they did search three homes in the 1100 block of Harding on Friday, the water was still too high to tell if any bodies were in any of these houses, so grab hooks were sent for. The guardsmen searched with the grab hooks but no bodies were found.

Relief Stations Serve Hundreds

[123] Refugees at Red Men's Hall.

The refugees who had been evacuated from School No. 16 were now housed in the Red Men's Hall and in the school attached to the Catholic Church of the Assumption of Father Weber. Over 10 were fed at the Red Men's Hall Thursday night. One hundred more spent the night at the church school. Father Weber took care of 16 of the weakest at his rectory attached to the church.

---

[123] *The Indianapolis Star*, April 1, 1913. Indiana State Library microfilm.

Provisions were now described as "plentiful".

By the end of this week, between 300 and 400 people had been fed daily at the church schoolhouse. There were eight Benedictine nuns taking care of the cooking and serving of the food. They issued food from their own stores for the first three days, before relief from outside came.

The Catholic school was the site of a temporary field hospital set up by the National Guard field hospital corps. There were three nurses there but no cases of serious illness.

Where Officials Direct Relief Work.

THE REV. JOSEPH F. WEBER.

MILITARY HEADQUARTERS AT HOME OF THE REV. JOSEPH F. WEBER, 1117 BLAINE AVENUE.

[124] The Indianapolis Star, March 29, 1913. Indiana State Library microfilm.

Status of Indianapolis' Bridges

PIER AND FRAMEWORK OF OLD VANDALIA BRIDGE.

125

The status of Indianapolis' bridges was as follows:

Bridges Wrecked

Meridian Street ($225,000 loss)
West Washington Street ($200,000 loss)
Raymond Street ($150,000 loss)
Vandalia Railroad Bridge (old one)
Indianapolis & Vincennes Railroad Bridge

---

[125] *The Indianapolis Star*, March 29, 1913. Indiana State Library microfilm.

Kingan's Private Bridge

Reported Weakened

Monon Bridge near Broad Ripple
Indiana Union Traction Bridge, north of Broad Ripple
Kentucky Avenue Bridge
Oliver Avenue Bridge
Morris Street Bridge

Police and National guardsmen were going to do a thorough house by house search of West Indianapolis this morning, in an attempt to get an accurate number of the dead. Captain Coffin and Captain Tyndall, of the Indiana National Guard led the party, which included Rabbi Morris M. Feuerlicht, Henry D. Danner and Representative Charles A. Corbly.

Today would be the first time mail delivery had been attempted in Haughville (a neighborhood west of the White River, roughly between 16th and Michigan Streets) and West Indianapolis. The post office planned on taking the mail over the White River via one of the standing railroad bridges. This would be the first delivery here since Tuesday morning. Mail began arriving in Indianapolis on Thursday. This included the first mail from the West, which had been on a Big Four train stopped outside of Indianapolis by the floods.

By the end of the day, mail was flowing into Indianapolis from trains from all directions, so this part of the crisis was resolved.

Sanitation and Disease Concerns

There were concerns about the spread of disease, specifically typhoid, in West Indianapolis due to the return of refugees through the numerous passes issued by Mayor Shank.

Sanitation in Indianapolis in 1913 was pretty bad, many houses, particularly in the flood zone of West Indianapolis having outhouses. Sewage was allowed to run directly into the White River, a situation which is only being corrected in 2017 with the building of a long-range tunnel system 200 feet below Indianapolis.

"Unless a skilled sanitarian is put in charge, there will be a terrible outbreak of typhoid, dysentery and other pernicious diseases of the intestinal system. These are epidemic affections and can and will spread with terrible rapidly," said Captain Boatman of the medical corps.

The area was beginning to already have a foul odor.

Friday, March 28, 1913, 9 a.m.

Water was restored in the mains by the Indianapolis Water Company today. Residents were warned to boil this water as it was unclean river water. There was a great danger of typhoid from drinking unboiled water.

The Relief Committee reported total contributions at about $37,000 at 9 a.m. today.

There was a great amount of anguish from family members looking for missing persons. Many people were separated from family members who were rescued.

Authorities did their best in this pre-computer age to post this information. The local papers printed full pages listing the names of those rescued.

The General Relief Committee had started an information bureau in Tomlinson Hall where accurate information on refugees could be obtained. By Friday ten girls using typewriters had entered between 3,000 and 4,000 names of rescued flood victims into an index.

A general phone number of 25000 would reach this bureau. Captain Coffin established his own bureau of information at his Belmont Avenue headquarters.

Several tons of donated clothing had been received by the General Relief Committee by now, which was now being taken directly to Tomlinson Hall. There, Mrs. Shank, Mrs. Joseph B. Kealing and Mrs. Irene V. Webb were in charge of sorting and distribution.

A number of people were driving automobiles and wagons around Indianapolis to collect this clothing. There were steps taken to prevent second-hand clothing dealers from getting to this clothing. Thursday night, a man wearing four pairs of pants was found by an inspector of the City Board of Health. He made him take three pair off, then he kicked him physically down a flight of stairs at Tomlinson Hall. He was allegedly a dealer.

Twelve squads of three men each were sent into the flood zones to make a survey of conditions and to take a census of survivors.

The city had employed a large force of men to work at clearing debris from west Michigan Street, west of the White River. They could reach the end of the street by auto, despite a layer of mud on the road.

Joe Mogue, superintendent of streets, sent out a call for 500 men to report Saturday morning to the street cleaning department at Kentucky Avenue and White River, to help clear the streets of mud and sand.

At present, 300 men and fifty teams of horses were working filling in the washed out approach to the Oliver Avenue Bridge and repairing damage along Fall Creek at Illinois Street.

Stories of survival were emerging from the refugees. John Thoma said he was one of dozens of people on the west side watching the rising waters opposite the Kingan & Company plant when they were cut off from their homes by the flood coming in behind them. This may coincide with the "wall of water" coming down Oliver Avenue from the west on March 25th.

He and a group of men were on the levee when someone yelled a warning from the north. A rush to escape followed and he felt many must have been drowned. Soon, he found himself followed by three men running close behind him. He was east of Belmont Avenue, on the Belt Railroad. He missed a step on the tracks and fell into deep water.

He struggled to get his footing and felt a cinder grade under his feet. Looking back, he saw the three men struggling in the water. He waited but did not see them reach safety. When he got to his home at 269 Minkner Street, it was under six feet of water.

Disaster souvenir postcards.

Spectators Interfere with Relief Work

Friday, March 28, 1913, 11 a.m.

At 11 a.m., Mayor Lew Shank and Superintendent of Police Martin Hyland issued an order opening the Morris Street and Michigan Street bridges opened to the public. This was a surprise to the city board of health. A rush of people into Haughville and West Indianapolis followed.

During this day, police and guardsmen estimated 30,000 people visited the flood zones. Those without a pass, including thousands of female spectators, viewed it from the east bank of the White River.

The barriers to entry were removed in part, because there was some ill feeling brewing, particularly at the Michigan Street Bridge and they thought a riot might occur.

Spectators gathered at Morris Street and Blaine Avenue on March 28, 1913.

"Everyone who approaches here without a pass breathlessly asks if any bodies are being brought out of the flood district," said an officer as he turned back an expensive auto filled with people, who had just made such an inquiry. There were rumors of hundreds of bodies being recovered and now

---

[126] *The Indianapolis Star*, March 29, 1913. Indiana State Library microfilm.

that the "recovery" process was supposedly started, people were coming out to see it. Traffic was heavy on the Michigan Street and Oliver Avenue bridges.

Superintendent Hyland issued orders to his officers today to investigate food prices in Indianapolis. Any jump in prices was to be reported to Hyland immediately. If Joseph B. Kealing, chairman of the general relief committee to investigate food prices found that increases had occurred, he would recommend to Hyland that these people be arrested on a charge of extortion.

A shipment of about 10,000 dozen eggs had arrived in Indianapolis that afternoon, a sign that the fear of famine in Indianapolis was greatly reduced. Fresh meat was still scarce, but local packing houses had several million pounds of smoked meats, enough to last the city for many weeks, on hand.

A Big Benefit Performance

Friday, March 28, 1913, 2 p.m.

Ina Claire   Pat Rooney

A "Big Benefit Performance" matinee was held at the English Opera House on the Monument Circle at 2 p.m. today. Over a dozen entertainers, including Pat Rooney, famous vaudeville dancer and Ina Claire, stage and film actress, performed in a show including dancing, comedy, music and singing.

Mayor Shank, who had much experience in Burlesque and performed a humorous monologue in vaudeville between terms as mayor, introduced the performers. Admission was $1.00 and all proceeds went to the flood sufferers.

The benefit was considered a great success, gross receipts being $1,686.15. A number of people paid up to $100 for seats selling for $1.00.

Another benefit for the victims of the flood was held this date at 2:30 at the Majestic Theater, in a musical comedy, "Frolics of 1913." The Indianapolis News published a list of the hundreds of people and companies contributing money for flood relief this date, which totaled $2,445.25 received March 26th. This money was turned over to the General Relief Committee.

Separately, $4,071.50 had been received by the General Relief Committee, for a grand total of $23,944.83. This is apart from the donation of clothing made by private companies and individuals.

Friday, March 28, 1913, 3 p.m.

The Board of Health Takes Control

At 3 p.m. today, the members of the city board of health convened a meeting to consider an order preventing all citizens from entering West Indianapolis.

As they sat down, hundreds of people were being carried by street cars over the West Michigan Street Bridge to the west side, after Mayor Shank and Superintendent Hyland had dropped the barrier to anyone entering the flood zones.

The statement issued after the meeting by Dr. T. Victor Keene said that the board of health intended to cooperate with the city administration to the utmost. However, they felt that allowing free and indiscriminate entry into these homes is a "greater calamity than the flood itself."

They adopted a resolution declaring that a quarantine existed in the flooded districts, calling for 100 special sanitary officers or policemen and requested 100 physicians to assist in the work ahead.

"Be it Resolved, That in view of the danger from possible pestilence or epidemic of disease arising from the flooded districts, this board hereby declares those portions of the city that have been flooded to be under a general quarantine and subject to quarantine regulations and laws until further notice."

127   Residents read the boil water warning.

The board of health printed several thousand large cards for posting around Indianapolis and several thousand more for distribution, which warned residents to boil all water and milk. Well water was also largely contaminated due to the flood.

---

[127] *The Indianapolis News*, April 1, 1913, p.9 – Indiana State Library microfilm.

The management of Crown Hill cemetery, largest in Indianapolis, announced they would donate graves for any bodies found in the flood zone. For persons of the Catholic faith, they would make arrangements for the body to be buried in cemeteries of that denomination.

Superintendent Martin Hyland

Martin J. Hyland had been superintendent of the Indianapolis Police Department since January 3, 1910. He had served the department since 1884 and was shot in the line of duty, March 17, 1902. During this catastrophe in 1913, he had not gone into

---

[128] 1913 IPD Yearbook, Lichtenberger History Room.

the field too often, having to stay close to his desk in headquarters.

He got his first real sleep in several days on Thursday morning and Friday he and his officers were getting a chance to take a breath as others could take the load off of them.

Hyland had pretty much been going 24-hours a day since Monday. He argued Friday that this disaster proved the need for a life-saving station along the White River, with two men and a good, heavy boat.

The police department then had two boats, neither of which was in good condition and in Hyland's words, "there is not one man in ten on the force who can operate them skillfully, especially on an occasion like this."

He described the steps he took when the crisis started. "When the first calls came for boats I made a hasty canvass of the force to learn if there were any of my men who could operate a boat. It was dangerous to permit a man unaccustomed to a boat to venture out into the swift currents. You would be surprised to know the few men out of the whole force who are acquainted with boats. Many volunteered.

I am exceedingly well pleased at the performance of the men. They have buckled to the work like good fellows and there hasn't been a complaint on account of the work they have been compelled to do.

"I am told that Capt. Coffin did not hesitate an instant at confiscating food supplies for the people marooned over on the West Side with him. The department and the board of public safety gave him full power to proceed as he saw fit, and I cannot see how he could have managed it better."

The men of the police department had taken up a collection for flood sufferers and it amounted to $500, with Hyland donating $25.

Friday afternoon, after a conference with local health officials, the mayor, and Hyland, it was decided that Hyland would take charge of all police, militia and city employees in the flood districts. Superintendent Hyland would also decide who was allowed access to the areas.

Superintendent Hyland immediately issued two orders. The first forbade any entrance to the flooded district unless you worked or lived there. The second was that home owners could visit and work on their homes during the day, but no one could spend the night there Friday or Saturday.

Hyland then had 12 detectives and eight mounted men west of the river to enforce these orders. In reality, few if any people trying to leave their homes were forced to do so. Police entreated them to leave for their own sake but if they refused, provided the resident with coal and returned to their duties preventing looting.

Cleaning up a City

When the water receded, it revealed a number of dead animals, including many chickens and some horses. Captain Coffin ordered a fertilizer company to come and pick them up. Others were burned in large pits along with other waste material.

[129] Bridge Street after it washed out.

---

[129] All They Had is Gone, March 1913 Flood. Indiana Historical Society, P0408

Residents of the damaged area, west of the White River was seen for the first time by many home owners. All of the furniture for a five block stretch of Washington Street was ruined. If it wasn't washed away it was water soaked.

[130] "Dozens of families were engaged in efforts to clean their furniture and make their homes habitable following their admission into the flooded territory. This picture shows two persons trying to get rid of mud that was left by receding water."

---

[130] *The Indianapolis News*, March 29, 1913. Indiana State Library microfilm

Four to five inches of mud covered everything and was soaked into the wood of houses. Women cried looking at their homes.

This morning on the porch of a home on North Harding Street, a widow sobbed, "I had just bought all my furniture new. I had worked for years to get enough money outside of living expenses to pay for this handful of stuff, and now it is all gone. No, it is not all gone, but I wish it were, for what's left is worse than nothing. It only reminds me of the happy little home I once had here."

There was one to two feet of mud on Bloomington Street, next to School House No. 16, now empty. The school was damaged by the rushing waters and a lot of debris was left behind. It was reopened however and was in use until low enrollment caused its closing in 1972. It is now the location of a church.

A nearby home was covered with mud and slime inside and out. A man shoveling mud out a parlor window was heard cheerfully whistling. His wife was humming the same tune while she pulled some rugs from the muck. She said, "Might as well laugh as cry. This is all we've got, but there's more where this came from!"

Friday, March 28, 1913, 5 p.m.

Captain Tyndall of the National Guard took steps to release a body of water held in an area known as "the pocket" by the I.&V. and Belt Railroad roadbeds in West Indianapolis. A section gang from the Belt Railroad dug trenches through these roadbeds and at 5 p.m. the backed up water rushed on its way to the river.

Houses moved from their foundations by the flood on Kentucky Avenue.

---

[131] Houses Moved from Their Foundations by Flood, Kentucky Ave., Indianapolis, Ind. March 1913, Indiana Historical Society, P0391

[132] Silver Avenue in West Indianapolis.

When the flood waters had receded, the night of March 28, Patrolman Atkins and Thomas O'Brien found Samuel Longworth, of 1423 West Ray Street, drunk on Sheffield Avenue near Market Street. He was taken to Captain Coffin's temporary substation at 244 North Elder Avenue.

Coffin was "very angry" when Longworth was brought before him and upbraided him for being intoxicated at a time when every

---

[132] From "Twelve Views of the Indianapolis Flood of March 1913" published by C.A. Tutewiler, authors possession.

man should be assisting others. He was taken from there to cell 13 at Police Headquarters.

Tonight, two train car loads of food and clothing was sent by the people of Indianapolis to flood sufferers of Dayton, Ohio. Dayton had probably suffered worse in this flood than any other city.

Friday, March 28, 1913, 10 p.m.

There was reported at 10 p.m. a rapid fall of the water level at Morris and Blaine Streets. Boats that had been floating at 3 p.m. that day were now dry docked. Fire Station No. 19 at Harding and Morris Streets, was expected to be back in use tomorrow morning.

Saturday, March 29, 1913

From William T. Riley's journal: *March 29. Pleasant sunshine. No work.*

Saturday, March 29, 1913, 6 a.m.

The Indianapolis Star published an editorial this morning critical of the lack of funds and response by the state government to the catastrophe in Indianapolis. "The state of Indiana has no contingency fund on which the Governor can draw for relief purposes."

Confirmation came in today that Chester Arnold, who vanished beneath the flood water at 4 a.m. Wednesday, was drowned. They hadn't found his body yet and planned on searching the area near the Belt Railroad where he was last seen.

Saturday, March 29, 1913, 12 noon

Temperatures in Indianapolis were mild this day, rising from 38 at 7 a.m. to 51 at noon. The forecast was for continued fair temperatures, a blessing for residents involved in the cleanup.

At Wulf's hall on Nordyke Street, a soup kitchen was opened. At noon, over 500 people were fed.

Total donations to the General Relief Committee fund as of today were $53,674.

Sunday, March 30, 1913

From William T. Riley's journal: *March 30. Warm, pleasant all day. Looked like rain in the evening. Went to work, got engine 1 at P.H. shop. Walked up town. No street car running on W. Indpls. Loaded dirt all day.*

Patrolman Nelson Granderson

"Almost 200 colored persons, driven from Haughville by the high water and cared for in the St. Paul Baptist Church on Sheffield Avenue, were able to return to their homes yesterday, but before going adopted resolutions thanking the persons who assisted them from their homes and who provided food. Special mention was made of

Patrolman Granderson, who worked in the neighborhood all night Tuesday."

The Indianapolis Star, Monday, March 31, 1913

Hettie Brewer

The African-American community had a mass meeting at the Bethel A.M.E. Church today, with Mrs. Martha A. Sissie presiding. They formed an organization to aid in the work of relieving the flood sufferers.

They appointed the following committee members: Mary E. Beck, vice-president, Daneva W. Donnell, recording secretary, Mrs. T.A. Smythe, treasurer, Mamie C.

Scott, Cora A. Jackson and Hettie Brewer, directors. Hettie became an early policewoman with the Indianapolis Police Department in 1922. A temporary relief station was established in School House No. 17 at 11th and West Streets, which served their community.

Today, Mayor Shank and Superintendent Hyland publicly thanked Sergeant Harry Franklin for his services in the flood district. They detailed the dangerous trip he took across the White River and through the overpass over Washington Street, which almost cost the lives of Cass Connaway, Billy Teubel and himself.

"Food supplies being unloaded in West Indianapolis."

Monday, March 31, 1913

From William T. Riley's journal: *March 31. Cool and windy. March goes out like a lion. Cool in the a.m. Calm after sundown. Clear. W. Indianapolis street car stopped March 25. 7 p.m. and again run March the 31st in p.m. Worked in pit loading dirt to fill in east at round house. Went to P.H. round house got engine no. 1, out for work 6 p.m.*

---

[133] *The Indianapolis Star, March 31, 1913.* Indiana State Library microfilm.

Patrolman Frank Giblin

After the receding of the flood waters, other IPD officers were able now to cross the White River into the stricken areas. There was a great need for relief workers to cook and distribute food and clothing to the survivors. One such officer was Frank Giblin, described as the "German comedian of the police department," who kept people loose with his wit while washing dishes at the Wesley Chapel.

As with any disaster, there were scam artists as they would be called today. They called them "repeaters" in 1913. People who received clothing and then came back for more.

William Harryman, one of the chief relief workers and secretary of the Relief Committee in West Indianapolis, came up with a system to prevent this today. Everybody receiving aid was placed on an alphabetical list which was referenced when someone came in for clothing.

There had not been any epidemics in Indianapolis, thanks to preventative measures. Today however, first responders were starting to get sick. Several officers were treated by physicians at a relief station. They treated 36 people and were going to be equipped with bicycles today.

Dr. and Mrs. J. Frank Potts, who resided at Blaine Avenue and Morris Street, turned their home into a hospital ward for 18 flood sufferers. They used every room for their patients. They had three nurses, Mrs. A.C. Pebworth, Mrs. William Cummings and Miss Jennie Trotcky, who has been mentioned previously for her relief work.

The nurses began working Wednesday and were still working through Sunday, March 30th.

Monday morning, the flood claimed another victim, when Mrs. Mary Pryor, age 38, died of exposure in the hospital. She had been rescued after being trapped in her River Avenue home when the levee broke on Morris Street.

Governor Ralston signed an order this night, recalling the National Guard, which was no longer needed.

The Death Toll

A list of the confirmed dead was finally published on March 31st. They were:

Mary E. Smith, 76, of 907 River Avenue. Her body was found the afternoon of March 30th in her home.

Mary Pryor, 38, of 1106 River Avenue.

Philip Reichart, 80, of 333 Beauty Avenue. He died of exposure at City Hospital Thursday from exposure.

A 7-month old son of Mr. & Mrs. Alec Olteon, 1007 West Morris Street. He died of pneumonia, contracted through exposure, on Thursday.

Chester Arnold, 19, 546 Alton Street, who drowned after trying to swim in White River Wednesday. His father wanted to go into the flood zone and search for his body but Captain Coffin overruled that and had Bicyclemen Gollnisch and O'Brien get grappling irons from headquarters and search today.

Mr. Philander R. Gray, 45, 1079 River Avenue, who disappeared in flood waters near Morris and Harding Streets Tuesday night, was found near the rear of IFD Station House No. 19 at Morris and Harding Streets.

The body was sent to the morgue. He had lingered too long moving furniture upstairs and was caught in a large flood surge after a levee broke at 10 p.m. March 25th.

The last victim was found by E.S. Graham, who was searching the area of Harding and West Washington Street. An unidentified man had floated to the surface in a pool of water.

Graham notified Bicyclemen Charles Gollnisch and Thomas O'Brien, who towed it to shore. They removed the body to the morgue, which was described as a male, about 30 years old. This body was later identified as Clarence Burns, rescuer.

134 J. Pierpont Morgan, financier, died the same week as Clarence Burns.

This was near where Burns was last seen when the canoe he and Charles Rogers were in broke in two in a heavy current on Washington Street, Tuesday at 9 p.m.

---

[134] *The Indianapolis Star*, April 2, 1913. Indiana State Library microfilm.

Burns disappeared, Rogers eventually was found alive.

Philander R. Gray and Clarence Burns were the 6th and 7th confirmed victims of the flood.

There was one man missing and presumed drowned. This was Johnny Johnson, 52, of 338 North Miley Avenue. He hadn't been seen since leaving work at the Vandalia shops just after the levee broke, at 6:15 p.m. He was wading toward the Belt Railroad, 15 minutes before an 8-foot wall of water would hit it from the other side.

Student Killed by Wire While Hunting Specimens

WILLARD RHOADS.

A search for zoological specimens was fatal Saturday to Willard Rhoads, a student of Shortridge High School. The young man stepped on a half-buried high tension wire while he and a companion were near the State Fair Grounds and was killed almost instantly. He was the son of Mr. and Mrs. C. S. Rhoads, 2403 North Pennsylvania street. The funeral will be held at 2 o'clock tomorrow afternoon at the home and the burial will be in Crown Hill Cemetery.

In addition, there was one accidental death attributed to the flood. Willard Rhoads, 19, 2403 North Pennsylvania, stepped on a live

---

[135] *The Indianapolis Star,* March 31, 1913. Indiana State Library microfilm.

wire while looking through some binoculars and was electrocuted.

There was one man listed among the "known dead" on Thursday, who made it known today that he was alive. George R. Smith, of 1651 West Michigan Street, appeared at Police Headquarters, Monday to correct that notion.

He said he had fallen off a boat in West Indianapolis Tuesday while rescuing a family. He remembered nothing from that moment until he woke up in Shelbyville Sunday. Police thought he was delusional.

This afternoon, what was described as the "first romance of the flood" resulted in a marriage. Harry S. Garrison and Miss Nina Moore, who found romance after evacuating their home Tuesday night, decided to get married as soon as possible.

Mayor Shank wed the couple in the office of the building inspector. The mayor accepted a fee of $1.00 which he promptly turned over to the General Relief Committee.

There was another flood related death recorded this night. A 3-week old baby in the Henry Taylor family, died of exposure. They lived in the flood district but were evacuated to 719 Maxwell Street. This was death number eight.

One death that was flood related, which came to light in the writing of this book was that of Frank Buchanan, an African-American male age 74. Buchanan suffered frost bite of the feet due to exposure on March 24th and he died of gangrene, 3:30 a.m., March 27th at City Hospital.

The Strain of Command

Superintendent Hyland paid a visit to Captain Coffin's headquarters at 244 North Elder Avenue March 31st. He saw that the full weight of the relief effort here was on Coffin's broad shoulders, the citizen's relief committee not having sent anyone to aid him. Hyland asked the committee for immediate aid, as they had apparently overlooked the area north of Washington

Street, while they concentrated on West Indianapolis, south of Washington Street.

Superintendent Hyland said that only the powerful physique of Captain Coffin was preventing a nervous breakdown. He felt Coffin was in no condition to be on duty and would be relief of the load as soon as possible. Days would pass before this would happen, however.

All of the special policemen on the west side were discharged from their duties on April 1st.

On Tuesday, April 1st, George W. Arnold identified the gray coat of his missing son Chester. It was found at Harding and Washington Street. The 9th known flood victim died of pneumonia today. She was Margaret Kuchler, age 9, of Mr. and Mrs. Peter Kuchler, of 426 West Raymond Street.

Captain Coffin ordered that no junk dealers were to be allowed in his district (north of Washington Street). He instructed his officers to have them brought to his headquarters at 244 Elder Avenue.

Superintendent Martin Hyland sent word out today that about 50 of the boats that IPD contacted for, were missing. He wanted their return, to avoid the department being charged for them.

It was known that there were a lot of boats that were stranded when the water went down and nobody had come to claim them. Thirty canoes that were furnished by a sporting goods store were missing. A dozen instances were known where they capsized and were carried away by the current.

Romance in the Flood Zone

REFUGEES PRINCIPALS IN WEDDING AT Y. W. C. A.

136 Left to right: Rev. A.B. Philputt, Christy Anderson, bridegroom; Ethel Krouse, bride; Miss Bernice Fuller and Miss Alma Sickler, Y.W.C.A. workers.

At the Y.M.C.A, one of the refugees was Miss Ethel Krouse, the young lady who lost her wedding dress when her Pearl Street home flooded. She was cheered when her bridegroom, Mr. Christy Anderson, arrived there was well.

Her mother and sister, who were separated from her when Ethel went back home to try

---

[136] *The Indianapolis Star*, April 2, 1913. Indiana State Library microfilm.

and save her wedding trousseau, were at the Manual H.S. refugee center.

The ladies at the Y.M.C.A., after finding out about Ethel Krouse's wedding dilemma, did their best to give her a bridal shower. Everyone wanted to give a gift. The wedding went on as scheduled, but at the "Y", the first ever held there.

First, the bride was led into the committee room where a large table was piled high with gifts. The 2 p.m. ceremony was conducted by the Rev. A.B. Philpott. Cake and refreshments were served afterwards.

A System of Relief Stations

MEN WHO DISTRIBUTE RELIEF IN HAUGHVILLE.

[137] Officers and men, with the exception of Police Captain George V. Coffin, who are stationed at relief substation in Haughville. The headquarters is at 244 North Elder Avenue.

Superintendent Hyland returned to police headquarters the morning of April 2nd, leaving Sergeant Franklin in charge of police operations on the west side near School No. 46, Howard and McClain Streets. At this point in the recovery effort,

---

[137] *The Indianapolis Star*, April 2, 1913. Indiana State Library microfilm.

the city had established these relief stations and substations.

Station No. 1 – General Headquarters for West Indianapolis, School No. 46. Sergeant Harry Franklin.

Substation 1a – Church of the Assumption, 1117 Blaine Avenue. Rev. Joseph F. Weber.

Substation 1b – Wulf's hall, Morris Street and Nordyke Avenue. Samuel E. Raub.

[138] Despite the length of time which has elapsed since the flood waters subsided, a long line of persons continually waited to enter the clothing distribution room in the relief headquarters in West Indianapolis.

---

[138] *The Indianapolis Star*, April 2, 1913. Indiana State Library microfilm.

[139] West side women waiting for opening of relief station maintained by Indianapolis Business Men's Association.

Substation 1c – Indianapolis Business Men's Assocation, 1239 Oliver Avenue.

Station No. 2 – West of the River and north of Washington Street, 244 Elder Avenue and Wesley Chapel; Captain George V. Coffin.

---

[139] *The Indianapolis Star*, April 5, 1913. Indiana State Library microfilm.

Substation 2a – Lauter Memorial building, Market and Greeley Streets.

140 Relief workers at Substation 3, 973 West New York Street.

Station No. 3 – District east of White River and north of Washington Street, 973 West New York Street.

---

[140] *The Indianapolis Star*, April 3, 1913, Indiana State Library microfilm

Substation 3a – Montcalm and 16th Streets. Charles L. Hutchinson.

District No. 4 – East of White River below Pogue's run, West Raymond Street and Bluff road. Mr. Bremen and Mr. Byers.

Mayor Lew Shank pitching in.

---

[141] Lichtenberger History Room. Indianapolis Star Magazine, April 7, 1953.

Captain George V. Coffin, was finally relieved of his flood duties, effective Saturday, April 5th. He was expected to return to his desk at headquarters the following Monday morning. Patrolman Thomas O'Brien, who worked side by side with Coffin during the crisis, described his management style, in his Irish brogue.

Thomas O'Brien

"Niver once did I hear him say, 'Officer, you go and do that!' By all the faiths it was always, 'Officer, follow me and we'll do that.'"

The Pool of Death

On Monday, April 7th, the body of John Johnson, 52 years old, of 338 North Miley Avenue, was found in a pool of flood water. It was located 100 yards south of the Big Four Railroad, east of Belmont Avenue. It was taken from the water to the morgue. Bernard A. Gallagher, conductor of a Big Four train, spotted the body floating on the surface.

John had last been seen on the railroad grade east of Belmont Avenue, trying to make his way home. His watch stopped at 7:10, about 40 minutes after the wall of water cut through the railroad grade.

One of the last of the known dead flood victims, that of Chester Arnold, 19, was recovered April 11th in the "pool of death" west of the Big Four Railroad crossing. He drowned Wednesday, March 26th.

He was the 10th confirmed victim. Arnold's body, the 3rd to be taken from this pool, was buried in mud, bushes and debris. The mud was five feet deep in places and he had been suspected of being in the pool for over a week.

Coffin Files a Complaint

William Milam

On April 8, 1913, charges of neglect of duty and conduct unbecoming an officer were forwarded to Martin J. Hyland, superintendent of police this date, against Sergeant William Milam of IPD.

This resulted from the report of Captain George V. Coffin on Milam's refusal to report for duty during the flood. Coffin stated that one night after the water receded, Milam reported for duty at Coffin's temporary headquarters, in civilian clothing.

Coffin asked why he hadn't obeyed his order, did he not know he was needed badly? Milam replied that his wife had been sick and he was in bad shape at home.

Captain Coffin refused Milam's help and ordered him to report to Captain Kruger at police headquarters, which he did. A report was submitted to the effect that Mrs. Milam had assisted in relief work at the church and did not appear to be sick. Milam was tried before the Board of Safety on April 16th.

During the hearing, it was brought out that the man who brought Coffin's message to Milam, said "They want you to come", not mentioning Coffin by name.

Milam stated he had no opportunity to leave the house until Wednesday, March 26th in the afternoon and that when he did leave, he immediately hunted up Captain Coffin and told him he would put on dry clothing and report for duty that night. However, he said he was unable to report for duty due to an attack of lumbago.

He also said he was ill at the time of the flood and had never tried to avoid doing his duty. He said he was "confused" due to the loss of property he had spent his life acquiring and "If I had it to do over again, perhaps I would have acted differently."

William Milam's personnel record indicates he was suspended for 30 days on May 14th for conduct unbecoming an officer. Milam retired in April of 1920, after 30 years with IPD. He passed away September 27, 1921.

The Flood Roll of Honor

On April 3, 1913, Captain Coffin made some public comments about the brave police officers and citizens who risked their lives to save their fellow citizens. He suggested gold medals be issued to these heroic first responders.

The idea caught on. On April 9th, the Board of Safety, which supervised the police and fire departments, issued an initial "Flood Roll of Honor". It was intended that more names would be added as their actions became known.

Among the names were those of these Indianapolis Fire Department firefighters:

Engine Company 14, 2960 Kenwood Avenue:

- Captain John Monaghan
- "Springer"
- "Statt"
- Fred Johnson
- "Bruce"

Hose Company 16, manned by African-Americans at 1602 Carrollton Avenue:

- Captain Clarence W. Miller
- John Logan
- William McGhee
- Claude C. Burris

Hose Company 19, Morris and Harding Streets:

- J.J. Monahan
- J.E. Zenor
- M.C. Dickson
- F.M. Quinn
- C.F. Leser

Truck Company 6:

- John McGinty
- J.E. Daugherty

Hose Company 18:

- E.J. Barnes

The author has taken the liberty of adding the names of the known boatmen, nurses and other police officers and firemen who quietly did their duty in the flood zone during this catastrophe.

Also listed are many men who had being listed on the "Flood Roll of Honor" mentioned in their obituary. The author believes the Flood Roll of Honor was to be a permanent record of these men and women, but over the years, it has been forgotten.

*There are many who during the recent flood, rendered invaluable
services to the city during their rescue work. Some are known, but a
very large number are unknown and unpublished.
The board of public safety of the city of Indianapolis takes this
opportunity to express its high appreciation of the Christian courage
and heroic valor exhibited by all who engaged in the rescue of their
neighbors from death and the flood.
We commend them for their heroism. It was good and great.
We hope that their conduct may always be remembered and to that end:
It is now Resolved, That names of all of those who are known to this*

board to have volunteered their assistance in the work of rescue shall be placed upon the following roll of honor.

Indianapolis Board of Safety

Police Officers

George V. Coffin	Harry Franklin	Charles Barmfuhrer
Charles Metcalfe	Frank Row	Othello Thomas
Bert Atkins	Joseph Klaiber	Harley Reed
Victor Houston	John Sheehan	Thomas O'Brien
Alfred Ray	Jesse Sanders	Leonard Forsythe
James Black	Nelson Granderson	Hanford Burk
George Cox	Frank Giblin	Joseph Fletcher
Herbert Fletcher	Samuel Young	Fred Judkins
Walter Cox	George Stone	John Repp
Edgar Hobbs	Charles Gollnisch	John Hostetler
K.A. DeRossette	Charles Johnson	
Benjamin Lansing	John Eisenhut	
Oscar Merrill	Thomas McCoy	
Richard Pressley	Guy Harper	
Jeremiah Doody	Herschel Gill	
Thomas Eisenhut	William Hansford	
Alvin Perry	William Wilson	

Firemen

Fireman John Ryan Sr.

John Logan	Clarence W. Miller	William McGhee
Claude C. Burris	Fred Johnson	John Monaghan
Charles Murphy	John Ryan Sr.	J.E. Zenor
M.C. Dickson	F.M. Quinn	C.F. Leser
E.J. Barnes		

Citizens

Cass Connaway	T.E. Jones	P.Q. Pendergast
Will Teubner	H.W. Wagner	Thomas Nelson
George F. Edenharter	E. Samuels	T.F. Reinor
George W. Beeman	E.V. VanHorn	R.D. Thomas
James Lampkin	Lemuel Christie	Morton Matthews
Jack Culp	Mayme Brennan	A.H. Lawrence
A Neville	W.D. Bartelle	A.M. Greiner
J.T. Moffatt	Joseph Weber	James Hixon
George A. Barton	Fred Robinson	Marion Forthoffer

---

[143] Indianapolis Firefighters Museum Collection

William R. Harryman	Morris Feuerlicht	Edward Brennan
William L. Reily	Harry Claffey	G.H. Westing
John F. Concannon	Clarence Atkins	Larry Dorrence
Joel Baker	William Reagan	Harvey Reed
Elton Hart	Henry Watson	Ralph McIntyre
William Wyman	Joseph Rodgers	E.L. Deitz
Charles Rogers	Clarence Burns	H.C. Tutt
Bunny Long	Albert Harris	S.S. Long
O.K. Downey	Harry Bly	Frank Hulse
Lorian Arnold	Mr. Nicholson	Ethel Trotcky
Solomon Trotcky	Mary Trotcky	Myrtle Trotcky
Jennie Trotcky	Ethel Conklin	Glenn Wells
L.C. Huddlelston	Howard Foster	John Taggart
Dan Healy	Noble Dean	Burt McDaniel
Otis Faust	Cecil Faust	Joseph Taggart
Happy Wirth	Harry Fehrenbach	Herbert Hyman
E.R. Hisey	George Caldwell	Willard Wymann
Jake Flick	George R. Smith	J.E. Settles
Edward M. Colla	Jack Cullup	James Lamkins
J. Frank Potts	Mrs. J. Frank Potts	Mrs. A.C. Pebworth
Mrs. William Cummings	Jimmy Burcham	Herbert Burcham
Patrick Hilroy		

1913 Flood photo. [144]

Flood Control

In the aftermath of the Great Flood of 1913, the planners of the city of Indianapolis resolved to take the steps needed to prevent this catastrophe from happening again. The White River had topped out at an estimated 29 feet above flood stage.

One more foot of water would have sent the flood over the east bank and flooded the Monument Circle and downtown Indianapolis. This would have caused an unbelievable loss in property, due to all the

---

[144] From City of Indianapolis webpage.

valuable goods in business basements being flooded.

A tall levee topped by a road was built in 1916-1917 on the west side of the White River, at a cost of $2.5 million. The proposal in 1923 was to spend another $7.5 million over five years to complete this project.

The bridges along White River, which were endangered, would be rebuilt or replaced. The Kentucky Avenue and Oliver Avenue Bridges were both replaced in 1925. Many pedestrian and railroad bridges would be extended, as one major problem during the flood was that the approaches to the bridges were either covered with water or washed out.

The remainder of the work, overseen by Harvey W. Cassady, chief of the flood prevention program, city engineering department, included:

- A levee and roadway built on the east bank of the White River. All levees

would be built 4 feet above the 1913 flood level.
- Dredging the White River, removing jutting lowlands and making the channel uniformly 650 feet wide and 33 feet deep.
- A wide bend in the river heading east will be eliminated north of Raymond Street, straightening it out.
- A concrete wall to be built on the east bank of the White River, identical to the one built in 1916-17 on the west bank.

It was believed that these improvements would make the swampy, useless land on the east bank attractive for real estate development, which is what happened to the west bank in 1917.

Epilogue

An examination of all local newspapers in April 1913 and death certificates for the period of March 25-28th indicate that there were 5 known drowning cases and the other 6 deaths were due to accident or exposure, making a total of 11.

The five drownings were the accepted total in 1952, but the Encyclopedia of Indianapolis gave the death toll as 25. Evidently the massive response of rescue boats prevented it from being much higher. Almost all of these deaths occurred in West Indianapolis.

However, it must be said that trained observers such as Captain Coffin saw unmistakable evidence of people drowning, such as bodies floating by in the water. These bodies and those of people passing through town who may have been washed down stream were never found. No one will ever know the true death toll.

Cass Connaway said after the flood that "I didn't do anything but handle the rudder. Anyone could do that." He was a judge advocate general of the Y.M.C.A. in France during World War I. He served as secretary of the Buffalo, N.Y. Real Estate Board for several years after the war. Connaway had been an attorney since arriving in Indianapolis in 1891. He died in Cleveland, Ohio, July 31, 1939 at age 70.

Billy Teubner (left) and William J. Teubner and Joseph Merkel after Teubner won the 10-Mile F.A.M. National Championship trophy at the old Point Breeze track in Philadelphia on August 13th, 1910.[145]

---

[145] http://archivemoto.com/thearchive/2017/11/2/archive-icon-william-j-teubner

Billy Teubner, Connaway's partner in the motor boat, said for his part, "I just watched the engine and kept going. That wasn't hard to do. Connaway and I owe lots of our success in rescuing people to Charley Foley, who stayed on shore and assisted us in keeping the engine in shape."

Teubner had been one of the best motorcycle dirt and clay track racers in the United States from 1908-1911. In a sport that saw 30 men killed during the 1913 season, Teubner decided to retire in March of 1912.

He then worked as a salesman for the Hendee Manufacturing Company, which is how he ended up climbing into a boat on the White River, March 25, 1913. Thanks to Archive Moto for the photograph and biographical material on this hero of the flood.

James W. Cline, the saloon keeper who kept working underneath his car as flood waters approached him on March 25th, survived the flood. He moved to 1428 North

Olney Street and became a salesman. He was struck by a car on Madison Avenue and died, November 13, 1928, aged 64.

Harry M. Franklin was born in Indianapolis in 1870. After the flood, he was promoted to the rank of Lieutenant on November 26, 1913. However, in one of the numerous political moves that affected the police department in those years, he was demoted in January 1914 to Patrolman. Franklin submitted his resignation. Influential citizens who witnessed his work during the flood protested this demotion.

In January 1918, he was reappointed to the police department with the rank of Captain. During World War I he always organized and led the parades involving the police department. He left IPD in 1921 and died February 14, 1935 in Indianapolis.

Charles P. Gollnisch, who was "chief" for a brief time west of the White River, served with the Indianapolis Police Department for 40 years, retiring August 20, 1941. He served as a detective for 20 years, figuring in a number of high profile cases. A native of Germany, he died December 23, 1944 in Indianapolis, aged 73.

Alfred Ray, who tried in vain to warn the residents along Fall Creek to evacuate, was promoted to Captain in 1917. He was nearly murdered on August 29, 1922 at Sullivan Park when stoned by a crowd of rowdies. This was due to him breaking up gangs of troublemakers in the park. Ray left the department in 1925 and died March 2, 1926 of a brain tumor.

Ethel May Krouse, who waded through flood waters to try and retrieve her wedding gown, did not remain married to her bridegroom, Christy Anderson. She remarried on January 22, 1919 to Claude Garvin. She died in Indianapolis, March 15, 1972, aged 75.

Harley Reed, who almost drowned in the White River March 25th, was promoted to Captain in 1919. After retiring in 1933, he came back to work as a detective sergeant from 1943-1947 during a manpower shortage. He died December 4, 1954 at Monticello, Indiana, aged 74.

Lieutenant Charles Barmfuhrer, who showed able leadership during the flood, served as Captain from 1913-1914, before becoming the first man to be appointed to the rank of Inspector of Police in 1915. He died while holding this rank, second highest in IPD, on July 6, 1917, aged 45.

Victor Houston, a patrolman who assisted in the rescue work at School No. 16, was promoted to Lieutenant in 1926. On March 26, 1928, he was critically injured when a police emergency vehicle collided with a car that failed to yield while on a burglary run, then crashed into a brick wall at 21st and Illinois Street. He recovered and retired in 1942. Houston died January 19, 1946 in Indianapolis, aged 60.

William R. Harryman, court official who spent the week being a volunteer assistant to Captain Coffin, was a well-known attorney after the flood. Active in local political campaigns, he was known as

"Admiral" Harryman to the police for his service as a boatman.

Harryman became ill with the flu late in 1922 and had been in poor health since then. Becoming despondent, his wife hid his revolver. A week later, he found it and disappeared. She called a family friend who was running to the home when he heard two shots. The body was found in the rear of the home. William R. Harryman was 41 years old when he died, July 24, 1923.

Father Joseph F. Weber, one of the true heroes of the flood, was a native of Morris, Indiana. He was ordained June 15, 1889 and was appointed assistant at St. John's church in Indianapolis.

He organized the Assumption Parish in Indianapolis in 1893. In the 43-years he served as pastor there, he organized many religious groups and was active in the west side community, organizing the Catholic youth. He received about 2,000 converts to the faith during that time.

Father Weber, who was friends with leaders of both political parties, appeared many times before the City Council. He was credited with obtaining better street car service and street improvements for the west side.

In 1933, a Chicago gangster named John "Jake the Barber" Factor had himself "kidnapped" with Al Capone's assistance, to avoid being extradited to England to serve 24-years in prison. Capone wanted to blame rival gangster Roger Touhy. Chicago Police understood that Father Weber knew Roger Touhy when the latter was a boy and had given him spiritual guidance in his home. They asked that he come to Chicago, which he did on July 7, 1933.

Father Weber arranged a meeting with Touhy at his home in Des Plains, Illinois, being driven there by one of his men. Roger Touhy told Father Weber, "Father, you know I'd never kidnap anyone. I have to guard my two boys night and day. If the syndicate ever laid hold of them it would mean the end of me. I couldn't kidnap anyone." Touhy offered to help solve the kidnapping as long as Weber set the meeting place with Factor. After a $75,000 ransom was paid, Factor was released July 12th. Touhy was set up in a secret police lineup and identified as one of the supposed kidnappers and arrested.

Father Weber was convinced of Touhy's innocence and said he had been "framed." He testified for the defense at his trial, January 31, 1934 in Chicago. It was later revealed that the kidnapping was faked and that corrupt prosecutors were behind the trial. Touhy spent 25 years in prison for the kidnapping and was murdered 22 days after his release by the syndicate.

Father Weber was well known to give his own money to the poor or victims of misfortune. He made arrangements for numerous people in trouble with the law for bail. Parishioners purchased a car for Father Weber. He had the car a few days and after paying for gas and oil, he said, "They bought me that car to keep me poor and humble. It's going to keep me broke, all right." Father Weber died July 13, 1935, aged 70, of cancer.

George V. Coffin, most visible first responder of the Great Flood of 1913, was respected and admired by the citizens of Indianapolis for his courage and common sense leadership. After Superintendent Martin Hyland resigned during a crisis in the department, Coffin was appointed his replacement, November 25, 1913.

He was demoted January 5, 1914 and resigned two weeks later. He had political ambitions and on November 6, 1914, was elected Sheriff of Marion County. Coffin was reelected in 1916 and resigned January 7, 1918, being appointed the Chief of the Indianapolis Police Department. One of the more historic moves that occurred during his tenure as chief was the appointment on June 15, 1918 of 14 policewomen, a first in departmental history.

He resigned August 1, 1919 from IPD and from 1920-1928 was head of the Republican Party and the local "boss" of politics.

George V. Coffin died April 10, 1938 in Indianapolis after a recurring illness.

Acknowledgements

The Indiana Historical Society for use of their images of the flood.

The Indiana Album for use of their images of the flood.

IFD Fireman Brian Killelia, archivist, for use of images from the Indianapolis Fire Department's museum.

Trudy E. Bell, longtime researcher of this catastrophe and author of *"The Great Dayton Flood of 1913"*, for her support when I began my own research.

www.ingramcontent.com/pod-product-compliance
Lightning Source LLC
Chambersburg PA
CBHW071258110426
42743CB00042B/1086